Six Steps to College Success

Six Steps to College Success

Learning Strategies for STEM Students

Kathleen C. Straker, M.Ed.

Eugenia G. Kelman, Ph.D.

Karista Press

Houston, Texas

Karista Press
SixSteps2@gmail.com
www.SixStepsToCollegeSuccess.com

Publisher's Cataloging-in-Publication Data

Straker, Kathleen C.

Six steps to college success: learning strategies for STEM students / Kathleen C. Straker, M.Ed.; Eugenia G. Kelman, Ph.D.
p. cm.
ISBN 978-0979847516 (pbk.)
ISBN 978-0979847523 (ebook)
Includes bibliographical references.

1. Study skills. 2. Learning. 3. Science--Study and teaching (Higher) --United States. 4. Technical education. 5. Education--Study and teaching (Higher) I. Kelman, Eugenia G. II. Title.

Q181 .S775 2014

620.0071/1 --dc23   2014916722

Book Production Team
Glenna Collett – Interior & Cover Design
www.glennacollettdesign.com
Christopher Edwin Nuzzaco/Shutterstock.com – Cover photo
Tammy Dubinsky – Illustrations

To Mom and Dad for teaching me about grit.

To colleagues and students who have become dear friends.

—KCS

Acknowledgments

We have again enjoyed the support and encouragement of many people.

We are grateful to:

> ❯ Dr. Dennis E. Daniels for inviting us to work with our first group of undergraduates.

> ❯ Faculty, Staff and Students of the Undergraduate Medical Academy. Your hard work and dedication to excellence are a constant source of inspiration.

> ❯ Patsy Cannon, MLS; Maria Aleman; Abrar Chowdhury, BS; Joyce Haley, MS; Rik Henrikson; Laura Kilgore, BS; Bao-Quyen Nguyen; Tran Nguyen; Abigail Norris; Jennifer Reiss; Reba Rios and Rick Straker, MS, for reviewing and commenting on drafts of this manuscript. Your comments and insights helped make this a better book. We, of course, take responsibility for any mistakes that may remain.

> ❯ Tasia Isbell, Miranda Nguyen, Carmen Purvis and Maria Ruiz, for letting us include some of their notes as examples in this book.

> ❯ The students who have attended our workshops and read our other books. Your enthusiasm, challenging questions, comments and insights are what make working with you so fun!

It is a joy and privilege to know and work with you all!

Contents

STEP TWO
Prepare to Get More Out of Lecture and Reading (Pre-read)   51

STEP SIX

Self-Talk   163

Prepare for Entrance Exams   201

Foreword: Oscar, Ariel & Tran

The book (and adventure!) you are about to embark on is the same journey I went on to discover how to effectively and efficiently study and prepare for any class, any exam, and any amount of material that needs "digesting." What you have in your hands is the "cheat sheet" to being successful in your undergraduate studies and even in studies beyond.

It is through these methods that I bypassed the stress others were experiencing during the semester (especially on test days), along with getting the proper amount of sleep.

Using these strategies I developed my personal memory retention technique that I call the "Octopus Method." The name came to me after going to a seafood market and watching octopi in their tank. If an octopus only had one, two or three tentacles on the ground, it was easily pried up and out the tank. When an octopus had all eight tentacles on the ground, it was much harder for it to be taken. That is how memory works. If you link a new concept to eight other already-known concepts, it will stick and be retained.

By applying the strategies in this book I was able to graduate from college with a high GPA and gain entry into medical school.

Get ready to learn how to learn.

Oscar Nguyen

My study habits in high school were good enough to earn decent grades, but far from stellar. I was comfortable with just getting by academically.

Everything changed when I started college. The academic demands were much more challenging. But it wasn't until I received some very poor grades that I realized I needed to change how I studied.

I attended the Six Steps learning skills seminar the next semester. I learned how important it was to be prepared for class, to read, to make good quality notes, to review, and to self-test. Slowly but steadily, I stepped out of my comfort zone and purged myself of my poor study habits.

I gained an understanding about the importance of time management. I viewed every class assignment as an opportunity to use my newly-acquired study skills. I began to see the fruits of my labor: my class performance improved, I earned academic scholarships, and consistently made the dean's honor roll.

The study skills that I learned have been invaluable. They continue to help me achieve academic and personal success. I believe that it is important to be honest with yourself. Never settle with just being "good enough." No matter where you are academically, there is always room for improvement.

Ariel Morrow

Like other college students, I take my academic career seriously. Being a pre-medical student, majoring in Biology, I volunteer, shadow, belong to a pre-medical society and work two part-time jobs while maintaining a good academic standing. It is rather overwhelming, but I figured out a way to handle all those tasks and still be an A student.

I always felt that I needed more than 24 hours in a day to complete all my tasks. Indeed, many students feel that way. Luckily, after reviewing the manuscript for, *Six Steps to College Success,* I realized what was wrong. In the chapter on keeping focused, I learned about internal distractions. Thanks to this book I have found a way to get rid of my internal and external distractions.

Since I always have a tight schedule it is important to me that the time scheduled for studying should only be used for studying.

I am amazed that this book is literally the only book I need for a successful undergraduate career. This is an all-in-one book. It not only talks about memory, sleep, nutrition, time management, procrastination, distractions, motivation and study strategies, but also provides step-by-step guidelines and exercises along the way for you to evaluate your progress.

I like how the book distinguishes the difference between taking notes and making notes because I feel it is very important to differentiate those two steps in the learning process. Moreover, the book describes when and how to use each type of chart while making notes. I find that very helpful in organizing detailed information in the easiest way—not only to memorize but also to review and self-test before exams.

The authors also mention each strategy's significance and effect on studying, backed up by research and the authors' well-known books. The section on self-talk was inspiring. It helped me recognize my own self-talk and make it more productive.

As a result, I am more confident in exams and school performance in general. We all need strategies to handle tasks more efficiently and effectively. Those strategies are right here in this book.

Whether you are a high-school student or a college student, consider this all-in-one book as a guide for your academic success.

Tran Nguyen

START **HERE**
Laying the Foundation to Success

Do you want to take charge of your own learning? Though our work has been primarily with students in STEM (science, technology, engineering, math), this book is for all students who are looking for a study system that is effective *and* efficient.

We originally developed these learning strategies for graduate, medical, dental, veterinary and nursing students. Those students often tell us, "I wish I'd known how to study like this when I was in college! My life would have been so much easier!"

For the last ten years we have been testing these strategies to see if they also work for college students.

They do! They are every bit as effective and efficient as they are with our graduate and health sciences students.

So, for those of you who are interested in learning how to set yourself up for success—both now and in the future—read on.

⟫ What Makes This Book Different?

1. Most study skills books offer general advice of the "spend more time" or "be motivated" variety. We offer a detailed, but easy to follow, system that shows you each exact step of a complete study plan. We provide exercises to get you actively involved in each step along the way.

2. Other study skills books provide little, if any, scientific background for the advice they offer. Our study system is grounded in an evidence-based approach to learning—from Ebbinghaus's work on learning and memory in the 1880s through the most current research findings.

3. This book is based on over three decades of experience in helping students succeed academically and in their careers and lives. In addition to the research literature, our own students tell us these strategies work. We have worked directly, in groups and one-on-one, with over 3,000 students. We use insights gained from working with a wide variety of students in this book.

4. These strategies work equally well for online courses and for traditional classroom settings.

5. The new field of Educational Neuroscience draws from the disciplines of education, psychology and neuroscience. We have been drawing from these same disciplines of study for over 20 years! Much of the recent research in educational neuroscience better explains WHY the strategies we've been teaching are so effective.

This study system will help you retain the information presented in your classes, textbooks and labs and will teach you to:

> Reduce stress by developing a manageable schedule

> Get the most out of lectures

> Use critical thinking to organize essential information

> Create highly organized notes for easy review and self-testing

> Recall and apply information for exams and laboratory work.

As a college student, you are making a big investment of your time and money. Economists at the U.S. Department of Labor have shown that earning a college degree is an excellent investment in your future career (http://www.bls.gov/emp/ep_chart_001.htm). If you follow our study system, you will be in a much better position to profit from your educational investment.

)) Studying For the Long Term

What Do We Know About Learning, Retention and Long-Term Memory?

Some people mistakenly believe that new technologies and electronic devices make storing information in long-term memory obsolete. While the devices we use to access information will continue to rapidly evolve, the strategies we use to learn and remember that information will move at a slower, more human, pace. In fact, having access to so much information makes it even more important to learn how to use our brains efficiently and effectively!

In order to promote higher forms of thinking (analyzing, evaluating, creating) instead of just recalling facts, Benjamin Bloom developed a classification system of different types of mental skills. It is called "Bloom's Taxonomy" and was updated in 2000 by Lorin Anderson, a former student of Bloom.

The strategies taught in this book (especially note-making) will help you move to the higher levels of thinking (analyzing, evaluating, creating) and help you remember information for the long term.

Figure 0.1 Bloom's Taxonomy: Cognitive Domain

Analyze   Evaluate   Create

Apply

Understand

Remember

Image provided by Wikipedia @
http://en.wikipedia.org/wiki/File:
BloomsCognitiveDomain.svg#file

Cramming, for example, does not put information into long-term memory. You may recall enough from your all-nighter to do okay on a test the next day, but chances are that crammed information will be forgotten soon after the test. This is not an efficient use of your time if you're going to have to re-learn the information later. Keeping a steady study schedule, on a daily and weekly basis, allows for quick, repeated reviews, which is what puts the information in your long-term memory. This is called the "spacing effect" and is well documented in the literature. (See Pavlik & Anderson in the references at the end of the chapter.)

In your everyday life, what information do you have in your long-term memory? What numbers, routes, passwords or facts do you easily remember? If you answer, "The ones I use the most," you are absolutely correct. Psychologists who study learning and memory have shown that going over information multiple times increases learning, memory and long-term retention.

More than a century ago, a German psychologist named Hermann Ebbinghaus described the process of forgetting. He called it the Forgetting Curve. He also showed that you can slow down the forgetting process by periodically reviewing the information.

Don't worry about running out of long-term memory in your brain. Our brain's storage capacity is so vast that cognitive

Figure 0.2   Ebbinghaus's Forgetting Curve

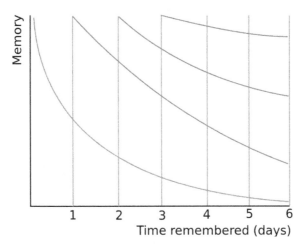

Image provided by Wikipedia @ http://en.wikipedia.org/wiki/File:ForgettingCurve.svg

scientists have not been able to measure how much information the brain can hold in long-term memory! (Clark, Nguyen & Sweller, 2006).

Students often tell us that they make an interesting discovery when tracking their study time. Students who spend their study time cramming often put in more hours of study, with unsatisfactory results. Students who have a systematic approach to their studies typically find they make better grades. Who wouldn't want to study fewer hours and get better grades?

How to Slow Down the Forgetting Process

The steps in this book show you how to slow down the process of forgetting by making it possible to periodically review and self-test on the information you want to remember. For example:

Step One: Schedule time to do the next three steps.

Step Two: Prepare for class.

Step Three: Create notes in logical patterns that are easy to review and self-test.

Step Four: Review your notes regularly between exams and self-test from your own notes or practice exams.

Step Five: Save time and remember more by learning ways to increase your concentration when studying.

Step Six: Keep calm when studying and preparing for exams by using productive self-talk and taking care of yourself physically.

The Learning Process

Learning is a process which begins with scheduling enough time for study, preparing for lecture, reading and interacting with the material by working problems or making organized notes. It then continues with reviewing and self-testing and culminates with the application of knowledge on a test. See the flowchart below.

Figure 0.3   Learning Process Flowchart

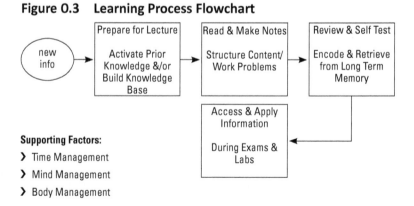

How Do These Six Steps Help You in College—
and the Rest of Your Life?

The secret to success in almost anything is taking small steps that will lead you closer to your goal. We have broken each of the learning strategies into easily applied components. If a step seems too big to you, break it down further.

There is a word for what the Six Steps teach you—**Grit.** Grit is also defined as perseverance or determination.

In recent years, Angela Duckworth has done extensive research in this area. In fact, she has developed a grit survey that only takes a few minutes to complete. If you would like to take a quiz to determine your current level of grittiness, go to http://www.authentichappiness.sas.upenn.edu/Default.aspx or use the link provided at end of this chapter in the References section under Grit Survey. The good news is that grit, like other characteristics, can be improved with deliberate practice.

These steps will also help you be successful in other areas of your life. As you go through the book, look for ways to apply these strategies to the rest of your life with family, friends, athletics and work. Being prepared mentally, emotionally and physically are important in all areas of your life and this book can help you develop those habits of success.

Maintaining Motivation

Some days your college experience will be more like a marathon than a sprint, so it is important to build in small rewards for yourself along the way in order to keep up your motivation. These rewards can be as small as having a snack, a verbal pat on the back, listening to a favorite piece of music or taking a walk. An evening getaway for a movie and dinner could be a larger reward. Plan these treats ahead of time and reward yourself when you've accomplished what you set out to do. Enjoy the fruits of your labor!

A secret to maintaining motivation is to learn to reward the effort. Don't wait until the end of a semester or even when an exam comes around. Reward yourself for preparing for lecture every day. Reward yourself for creating a beautiful set of study notes. Reward yourself for putting in the number of study hours you need each week.

The main thing to keep in mind about rewards is that your reward should not get you off track in your studies. Just as a dieter should not be rewarded for losing ten pounds by eating an entire carton of ice cream, neither should a student be rewarded for a good exam grade by missing the next few classes. Choose a reward that will keep you on track with your goals and that you can enjoy guilt-free!

Keep your rewards short and sweet and enjoy them frequently!

List three small activities you can use to reward your study activities this week.

Study Activity   **Reward**

_____   _____

_____   _____

_____   _____

⟫ How to Use This Book

The beginning of a course is the ideal time to start using the strategies we teach, but if the course has already begun, go ahead and start with the weekly plan below. It's much better to get started part way through the semester than to wait until an entire term passes by. It will take you about six weeks to work through the material in this book. Since this is meant to be interactive, it will not be helpful to just read without doing the quizzes and exercises. After the exercises, you will analyze your own experience and decide which permanent changes in your study strategies will lead to the greatest success—and decide if you are willing to make those changes. The sequence of topics is carefully designed, so we don't recommend skipping around the chapters your first time through.

Scheduling time is first, because you can't accomplish the rest of the system unless you have scheduled enough time. Pre-reading comes second, because it is the next step in the system we recommend. You get the idea.

Week 1: Read and complete the exercises in Start Here and Step 1, Time.

Week 2: Read and complete the exercises in Step 2, Prepare for Class.

Week 3: Read and complete the exercises in Step 3, Read and Make Notes—and continue practicing time management and preparing for class. Take your time in going through this step. Note-making is crucial to this entire study system.

Week 4: Read and complete the exercises in Step 4, Review and Self-Test. This is the last component of our study system. The rest of the book consists of information on how to improve your ability to use the system.

Week 5: Read and complete the exercises in Step 5, Keep Focused.

Week 6: Self Talk is Step 6. These are methods for increasing motivation and decreasing test anxiety.

After week six, evaluate your new study system. Make adjustments if needed, reward yourself for positive changes made—and keep up the great work!

We've included a bonus section on how to apply *Six Steps* to preparing for classroom and standardized exams. If you are planning to pursue graduate studies, this section can help you get ready for your entrance exam.

❯❯ Current Study Strategies

Take a few minutes and briefly describe how you currently study. How do you prepare for classes and/or exams? When and where do you do it? Be as detailed as the space allows.

_____

_____

_____

_____

_____

_____

_____

_____

_____

_____

After you complete this workbook we'll ask you to return to this section so you can evaluate the changes you have made in how you approach your studies.

> This study system works—if you work the system. That means completing the exercises— not just reading the book.

⟩⟩ Summary

The steps we teach will help you learn information for the long term and will help you accomplish what you need to in an effective and efficient manner.

Until we become a paperless society we are going to assume that you will be using both paper/pen(cil) and digital devices while studying and learning material, so we will address the pros and cons of each as we continue.

We welcome you on this path of discovering the most effective and efficient strategies for learning and memory. These strategies have been used successfully by thousands of students in professional and graduate studies and we are confident that they will be useful to you as well.

Get in.   Get through.   Get out.   Get going!

⟩⟩ References

(So You'll Know We Didn't Make This Stuff Up!)

Anderson, L.W. (Ed.), Krathwohl, D.R. (Ed.), Airasian, P.W., Crui-kshank, K.A., Mayer, R.E., Pintrich, P.R., Raths, J., & Wittrock, M.C. (2001). *A taxonomy for learning, teaching, and assessing: A revision of Bloom's taxonomy of educational objectives.* New York: Longman.

Anderson, a former student of Bloom, and others, revisited the cognitive domain in the learning taxonomy and made some changes, the two most prominent ones being, 1) changing the names in the six categories from noun to verb forms, and 2) slightly rearranging them. Link to graphic: http://en.wikipedia.org/wiki /File:BloomsCognitiveDomain.svg#file

Clark, R., Nguyen, F., & Sweller, J. (2006). *Efficiency in learning: Evidence-based guidelines to manage cognitive load.* San Francisco: Pfeiffer.

The guidelines in this book are based on more than 25 years of research conducted by John Sweller and his associates. Application of the cognitive load theory leads to efficient learning by minimizing or eliminating irrelevant material and emphasizing that which is relevant.

Duckworth, A.L., Peterson, C., Matthews, M.D., Kelly, D.R. (2007). Grit: Perseverance and passion for long-term goals. *Journal of Personality and Social Psychology,* 9, 1087–1101.

These findings suggest that the achievement of difficult goals entails not only talent but also the sustained and focused application of talent over time.

Duckworth, A.L. & Quinn, P.D. (2009). Development and validation of the Short Grit Scale (Grit-S). *Journal of Personality Assessment,* 91, 166–174.

Among adults, grit was associated with educational attainment. Among adolescents, grit predicted GPA. Among cadets at the United States Military Academy, West Point, grit predicted retention. Among Scripps National Spelling Bee competitors, the survey predicted final round attained.

Ebbinghaus, H. (1913). *Memory: A contribution to experimental psychology.* (Translated by Henry A. Ruger & Clara E. Bussenius; original German work published 1885). New York: Teachers College, Columbia University.

Ebbinghaus was one of the first scientists to study learning and forgetting. His work has withstood the test of time and is still often quoted.

Eliot, J. (2004). *Overachievement: The new model for exceptional performance.* New York: Portfolio.

The author has done field work observing and interviewing high performers and now advises clients on how to use stress to their advantage to perform at the highest level possible.

Foshay, W.R., Silber, K.H., & Stelnicki, M.B. (2003). *Writing training materials that work.* San Francisco: Jossey-Bass/Pfeiffer.

This guide is based on current cognitive psychology and instructional design theory and research. It addresses creating instructional materials, which is the same task that students must undertake when they make their own study notes.

Gerson, R.F., & Gerson, R.G. (2006, June). Effort management. *Training + Development,* American Society for Training and Development, pp. 26–27.

Research in attribution theory and motivation indicates that rewarding both effort and achievement induces people to be more willing to do a task again and even take on more difficult challenges.

Grit Survey. To take the survey, registration is required, but it is free. Look under "Engagement Questionnaires." The Grit Survey measures the character strength of perseverance. http://www.authentichappiness.sas.upenn.edu/Default.aspx

Maurer, R. (2004). *One small step can change your life: The kaizen way.* New York: Workman Publishing.

Maurer suggests the following actions to bring about change: ask small questions, think small thoughts, take small actions, bestow small rewards, identify small moments.

Pavlik, P.I. and Anderson, J.R. (2008). Using a Model to Compute the Optimal Schedule of Practice. *Journal of Experimental Psychology: Applied.* Vol., 14, No. 2, 101–117.
DOI: 10.1037/1076-898X.14.2.101
http://server-1.optim.cs.cmu.edu/people/Articles /2008%20Pavlik%20Anderson.pdf

U.S. Department of Labor. Bureau of Labor Statistics. (2013). Earnings and unemployment rate by educational attainment. http://www.bls.gov/emp/ep_chart_001.htm

Scheduling Your Time for Success

(WEEKS 1 & 2)

QUIZ How Do You Use Your Time Now?

Directions: Circle the number that best describes how you use your time during the school term. (No one will see these answers—unless you share them—so be honest.)

Yes / True	Sometimes	No / False	
0	1	2	**1.** Important tasks and due dates are recorded in my calendar.
2	1	0	**2.** I take a break from studying for a few days right after an exam.
0	1	2	**3.** During an hour of study, my break is 10 minutes or less.
2	1	0	**4.** I find myself running late for classes, appointments or other activities.
0	1	2	**5.** I get at least 7–8 hours of sleep most nights.
2	1	0	**6.** Friends or family often interrupt my study plans.

0 1 2   **7.** I carry study materials with me so I can study during small bits of time that might otherwise be wasted.

2 1 0   **8.** I wait until I'm in the mood to begin studying.

0 1 2   **9.** I spend close to one hour in personal study for every hour of lecture I attend.

0 1 2   **10.** I exercise at least two or three times a week.

_____   **Total Score** (sum of circled numbers)

FEEDBACK on Time Usage

1. Why waste mental energy trying to remember all the details of your daily schedule instead of writing them down? It's much easier and less stressful to write down what you need to do and then check it off when it's done. Of course you'll have to check your schedule every day—that's the whole point!

2. With a steady study schedule you can eliminate the stress and fear that come with falling behind. Get right back on your study schedule after an exam!

3. Study during your scheduled study time. A short break is good, but don't allow yourself to overextend your break. Never count an hour as an hour of study unless you actually study at least 50 minutes of it. See the section on ultradian rhythms for exceptions to this rule.

4. Being on time is the sign of a well-managed schedule. If you are running late, you may be over-scheduling, not being realistic in making time estimates, not consulting your

schedule on a regular basis or not looking forward to the event. Faculty members appreciate professional behavior, which includes being on time. In some classes it can even affect your grade.

5. If you answered "yes" good for you! Being sleep deprived is actually a waste of time because: 1) consolidation of information takes place while you are sleeping; 2) if you are not fully awake and alert in class or while you are studying you'll have to spend more time re-learning the information later. Also, according to recent research, not getting enough sleep can lead to 3) increased levels of stress; 4) a depressed immune system and 5) overeating.

6. It's hard to put friends off, but these situations give you the opportunity to practice setting boundaries. You can save your schedule by setting a date to meet that person at another time to spend some time together. If you let other people encroach on your time, you may come to resent them, so don't get started down that road.

7. Always carry something to study. This is easy to do if you can access your notes on your phone. Step 4 (note-making) offers suggestions about what notes are convenient to carry with you. Using little bits of time, frees up other time. Brief reviews are a gift of time—and a great way to get information stored in your long-term memory.

8. In your future career you will not have the luxury of going to work only when you "feel like it," so do yourself the favor of learning how to be in a good mood while you do what you have to do anyway. Step 6 can help you with this.

9. Good! You should spend one to two hours in personal study for every hour of lecture.

10. Use physical exercise as part of your recreation. You can even combine social activities with exercise by walking, hiking, running or playing tennis with a friend.

SCORE INTERPRETATION Time Usage

If your Total Score on these 10 questions is in the **0–5** range, you don't need to spend much time on this chapter. You're a very good time manager. Begin the Baseline Time Sheet exercise and see if you can pick up a few tips in the rest of the chapter.

If your score is in the **6–10** range, you have a good idea of what you should be doing but need to improve. The exercises in this chapter will help you better manage your time.

If your score was **above 11,** time management may be the key to your success! You need a better schedule before you can implement the Six Steps system.

)) Track How You Use Your Time

The purpose of this chapter is to help you create a schedule that allows one to two hours of personal study for every hour of lecture, depending of the difficulty of the course. This study system has been extremely successful for the students who adopt it, but you must schedule enough time. (Note: Though we use the term *semester,* the same ratio of 1–2 hours of personal study for every 1 hour in class, applies to *trimester* and *quarter* systems, too.)

If you are not spending enough hours in study, all the study techniques in the world will be useless. You must dedicate the time required to learn the material. Given that fact, what will your schedule look like?

As we mentioned earlier, full-time college students are typically scheduled for about fifteen credits per semester. The usual expectation at this level of education is that one hour in the classroom requires about one to two hours of personal study time

(U.S. Department of Education, 2011). So, a full-time student can expect to spend a total of about 30–45 hours each week in both scheduled class time and personal study time. Much depends on the type of courses you are taking. If you are in one of the more difficult majors (like STEM fields), expect to spend even more time in some of the upper-level courses.

What about Online Courses?
The same principles that apply to succeeding in the traditional classroom also apply to doing well in online courses. In fact, the time planning and management element becomes even more vital because less structure is imposed on your time. Even if you won't be sitting in a traditional classroom for your courses, the strategies in this book will help you achieve your academic goals.

How to Decide if an Online Course Is Right For You
The primary benefits of online courses are the reduced cost, drive time and being able to do your work when and where it is convenient for you. But there are also disadvantages, especially for students who are under-prepared, lack effective time management skills or do not have regular computer and internet access (Jaggars, 2014).

Some questions to ask yourself:

> Do you currently manage your time well?

> Can you stay motivated even when the work is difficult?

> Are you willing to contact the instructor when you need help?

> Are you able to commit one to two hours of personal study for each hour in the online class?

> Do you communicate well in writing?

> Are you skilled in using a computer for internet searches and word processing?

> Will you have regular access to a computer and the internet?

If you answered "yes" to all of the questions above, then an online course may be a good choice. If you answered "no" to two or more of the items above, you may want consider taking an online not-for-credit class, to see how you do. Rob Jenkins (2012), states that "sitting at home, alone, in front of their computers, with little in the way of emotional support—not to mention, in many cases, educational support" may not be such a good idea for some students.

If possible, talk with other students who have already taken the online course you are considering. If they say, "I thought it was great!" or "It was awful!" see if you can find out *why* they thought that. The reasons that made them like a course ("I could go to class in my pajamas") or dislike a course ("too much reading" or "had to take exams at a proctored testing site") may, or may not, matter as much to you. If, however, they say that the instructor was not clear in what was required, kept changing grading criteria or lost assignments on a regular basis, take note.

Some students have told us that they have forgotten that they had signed up for an online course! To prevent this from happening to you, make sure you schedule time in your planner every week to stay current in your online assignments.

The Minnesota State Colleges and Universities and the Georgia Department of Education websites have even developed quizzes to help you think through taking an online vs. a face-to-face course. The links to these two quizzes are: http://www.mnscu.edu/online /distancelearningquiz.php and https://registration.gavirtualschool .org/registration/survey.aspx

A final note regarding online courses: While sitting at your computer you may be tempted to visit sites unrelated to the course. In her book, *Finding Your Focus Zone*, Lucy Palladino writes, "The Internet has no last page." This is a simple reminder that it is easy to lose track of time while surfing the web. Some students find it helpful to block themselves from certain sites during class, to lessen the temptation of distraction.

Get a Baseline of How You Spend Your Time Now

Students often say, "There isn't enough time to do everything I need to do!"

About half of the students who begin our study skills course report that they spend ten hours or less per week in personal study, which is not enough to succeed, if you are carrying a full course load.

Faculty members tell us that many students do not, for varied reasons, dedicate enough time to their studies and are not prepared for classes or exams. Realistically, is there enough time to combine adequate study time with your other responsibilities at home and at school?

Act & Analyze

Exercise 1

Estimate How You Use Your Time

Let's do the math:	Average	Your Estimate
Available hours per week	168 hours	168 hours
Average time spent per week in class	15 hours	_____ hours
Number of hours suggested for personal study per week	15–30 hours	_____ hours
Sleep (average of 7–8 hours per night × 7 days)	49–56 hours	_____ hours
Everything else!	67–89 hours	_____ hours

If that sounds like plenty of time for exercising, relaxing, having fun with friends and family, eating, etc., here are some additional factors to throw into the calculation:

> Do you commute? How many hours per day or per week?

_____

> Do you belong to school organizations or participate in activities? How many hours per week do these involve? _____

> How much time do you spend with friends and/or a significant other? _____

> How about maintenance activities like personal hygiene or doing laundry? _____

All these activities take time, but often go uncounted. Keep track of *all* your activities to get an accurate record of your time. If you follow our recommendations for time management in this chapter, you will find time you would otherwise lose.

Now let's do a reality check. For the next week, we'd like you to keep track of where your time really goes. Follow the directions in Exercise 2 below.

Act & Analyze

Exercise 2

Reality Check. How Do You Really Use Your Time?

Most people do not have an accurate idea of how they use their time. The only way to find out is to keep track of it. This is where you get to be both the scientist and the subject. Use the following form to record your activities for the next week, or you may use the links listed in the references at the end of this chapter or even create your own version. Tally the numbers by category to see how you are using your time. By being totally honest in completing this exercise, you will probably discover wasted bits (or huge chunks) of time that can be converted into more productive activities. You may even find some "play time" that you didn't realize you had!

Download a time-tracking app or carry a Time Recording Sheet with you for the next week. You may want to fill in all your scheduled activities first—classes, regular meetings, work, commute, religious services or appointments to which you are already committed.

Record your activities in one hour units using the categories below:

> Lecture (LEC)

> Laboratory (LAB)

> Personal Study (PS)

> Maintenance (M)—include chores such as cleaning, personal hygiene, laundry, financial aid, shopping for necessities, etc. Note: Any shopping that is "fun" is R&R.

> Paid Employment (Job)

> Commute (COM)

> Physical Exercise (PE)

> Sleep (S)

> It may not seem fair, but count everything else as rest and recreation (R&R).

A full-sized version of the worksheet is available for download from our website: www.VitalStudySkills.com/worksheets

Worksheet 1.1 Blank Time Recording Sheet

Record your activities in ½ hour or 1 hour units for one week. At the end of the week calculate totals for major activities using the following categories: **LEC** (Lecture), **LAB** (Laboratory), **PS** (personal study), **M** (maintenance activities including shopping, cleaning, errands, eating, personal hygiene, etc.), **COM** (commute time), **Job** (paid employment), **PE** (physical exercise), **S** (sleep), **R&R** (rest and recreation, including anything that does not fit into previous categories).

	Mon.	Tues.	Wed.	Thurs.	Fri.	Sat.	Sun.
5:00 a.m.							
6:00							
6:30							
7:00							
7:30							
8:00							
9:00							
10:00							
11:00							
12 noon							
12:30							
1:00							
2:00							
3:00							
4:00							
5:00							
6:00							
6:30							
7:00							
8:00							
9:00							
10:00							
11:00							
12:00							
12:30							
1:00 a.m.							
2:00							
3:00							
4:00							
Daily:							
LEC							
LAB							
Job							
P Study							
COM							
Maint							
P E							
R&R							
Sleep							

Weekly totals: Lecture =_____ Lab = _____ Job = _____
Personal Study =_____ Commute = _____ Maintenance =_____ PE =_____
R&R =_____ Sleep =_____

While you are recording your time this week, read and do the exercises in Step 2, Prepare for Lecture. We often call preparing for lecture "pre-reading." Pre-reading a quick preview of the material you will be required to read later—and is a real time-saver. Adding this new study skill will make lectures more interesting, speed up your reading, increase your understanding and give you a head-start on making a good set of notes.

Go to Step 2—Prepare for Lecture. Return to this page after recording your time usage for seven days.

Analyze & Adjust
Check-Up for Exercise 2
Time Recording

Answer the questions below after recording your time for one week.

1. What did you learn about how you use your time?

   _____

   _____

   _____

2. How many hours did you spend in classes and labs each week? _____ hours

3. How many hours did you spend in personal study each week? _____ hours

4. How does your total compare with the recommended 30–45 hour per week average for a full-time student—or 1 to 2 hours of personal study for every credit hour?

   _____

   _____

   _____

5. How many hours did your sleep average per night?

_____ hours per week night   _____ hours per night on
weekends

6. Maintenance activities_____ hours per week

7. R&R (rest & recreation)_____ hours per week

8. Now compare these figures to your estimates in Exercise 1
and write your findings below. Were your original estimates
close to how much time you actually spend on these
activities?

_____

_____

_____

_____

9. Are there changes you would like to make based on what you
have learned thus far? If so, list one or two of the more
important changes:

_____

_____

_____

_____

Note: If you are not pleased with how you spend your time, take a
few minutes to reflect on the cause. Have you forgotten to build
in rewards for yourself? Have you overcommitted? Are you sleep
deprived?

_____

_____

_____

_____

)) Take Charge! Create Your Own Schedule

Planning Study Time

Now that you have a better idea of how you actually spend your time, you are ready to make some important decisions about planning a good schedule. Block out times for personal study when you can concentrate for at least an hour. Two hours would be even better. Aim for at least one concentrated study session every day. Schedule this block of time when you can be reasonably certain not to be interrupted. If you think two hours at a stretch is too long to maintain your concentration, work up to it gradually. Start with at least thirty minutes of study time, then increase the amount of time you study by 15 minutes per week until you are able to study for one and a half to two hours at a time. Focusing your attention is a learned skill. (See Step 5, Keep Focused, for ideas to help you increase your concentration and endurance.)

Taking a short break for refreshment and vigorous exercise during a study session will help you extend your period of concentrated study. And remember that a concentrated study period does not have to mean all that time is spent on one topic or activity. It just means that the time is dedicated to studying—pre-reading, reading, note-making, reviewing or self-testing—and nothing else. Maintenance activities and R&R should be planned for time when you feel less mentally energetic or need a break from an intense period of study.

These recommendations are based in the research on ultradian rhythms (Figure 1.1). During the day our bodies cycle through 90–120 minute periods of alertness with 15–20 periods of fatigue in between. At night these same periods correlate with deep sleep (90–120 minutes) and light sleep or wakefulness (15–20 minutes).

Figure 1.1 Ultradian Rhythms

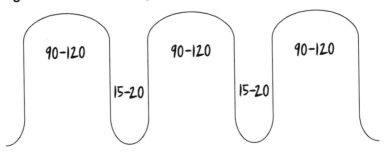

A simple way to schedule your study periods and breaks is with the formula below. For every 30 minutes of study, plan to take a 5-minute break before returning to another period of study. Many students use apps based on the Pomodoro Technique® to help them track their study time and breaks.

Chart 1.1 Study & Break Times

Minutes of Study	Minutes of Break	Minutes of Study
30	5	30
60	10	60
90	15	90
120	20	120

When possible, plan to schedule a study period soon after lecture while the ideas are still fresh in your mind. It will be easier to consolidate your notes and compare information from the lecture to the syllabus, textbook or handouts over the same topic. That's not always possible though, so do your best to plan a study period within 24 hours of that day's lecture. The longer you wait, the more time you'll have to spend re-learning the material.

If your lectures are in a long block, try to pre-read immediately before the block. For example, pre-read the evening before for a morning block, or at noon for an afternoon block. Pre-reading may seem like a waste of time until you actually start doing it. Once you are a pre-reader, you will find it saves time by making lectures more meaningful and helping you create a better set of notes.

Special Note About Online Courses

Online coursework typically requires additional time management skills as the courses often impose less structure (no classroom setting) and more flexibility. This lack of inherent structure requires that the student create his or her own structure and timelines to make sure the work is done in a timely manner.

Scheduling Study Periods

When to schedule your study time is an individual decision, but many students tell us that they are better able to concentrate in the mornings and early evenings, rather than closer to bedtime. Weekends should also become part of your regular study routine. Many students find, especially as classes become more challenging, that they must dedicate at least four hours to studying on weekends. Any work not completed during the week will need to be completed during the weekend. If you value having free time on weekends, make sure your schedule includes enough study time each day during the week.

Exercise and Study Breaks

Aim for at least thirty minutes of exercise every day. And yes, that long walk to and from your car or your dorm room counts! Using weights or weight-bearing machines at the gym may be an efficient way to get a good workout. Even simpler is learning to use your own body weight in exercises such as push-ups, pull-ups, squats and walking or running stairs.

In addition to regular physical exercise, it's important to give yourself short refreshing breaks between long study sessions. For example, playing the piano, listening (or dancing) to music, taking

a short walk, enjoying a period of meditation or inspirational reading are all useful rewards for a good study session. Even putting a load of laundry in to wash will get you up and moving around. Bet you never thought of doing laundry as a break!

Another idea for a break is to step outside, take a few deep breaths and be mindful of the day, the weather, the sky, trees, birds, all the life around you. It can be quite refreshing and energizing. These activities can slow down your busy thoughts and allow you to think about the bigger picture of your life and even motivate you toward your long-term goals.

Notice that most of our recommendations are for active breaks spent moving around. Studying can be very passive, so find a reason to get up and move around during breaks.

Guidelines: 1) During a break, do something *very different* from what you've been doing. That way your body and mind will know you've had a break. 2) Set a timer for how long you plan to take a break. Time passes so quickly that without a timer your 15-minute break can easily stretch into an hour.

Managing Your Schedule

Managing your time is a habit. Behavioral scientists tell us that the best way to develop and control habits is to use continual feedback until your new habits become established routines. So continue to keep track of your time as you move on to the next set of worksheets and exercises.

You will probably need to tweak your plans as you go along. You can't tell your brother that his emergency surgery doesn't fit into your schedule! When the unplanned happens, the lost study time needs to be made up. This make-up time will likely come from previously scheduled R&R or maintenance activities.

We suggest that you swap time only within the same week. Why? If you have a tight schedule, you probably won't have the time to borrow from next week. That's the slippery slope that leads to cramming, lost sleep and disappointing grades.

If you often find yourself having to borrow or swap time, take another look at your schedule. Are you unrealistic in estimating how long things take? Do unplanned activities interfere? Do some investigative work to find out what needs to be changed—and change it!

It is normal to make adjustments to your schedule during the semester. Each semester will require the creation and fine-tuning of an entirely new schedule. But each semester you will learn how to better use your time. It is a life-long process. You are off to a great start!

Plan Enough Time for Sleep

Much research has been conducted on the psychological and physiological effects of lack of sleep. Not surprisingly, the research shows that sleep loss impairs learning and memory. Sleep research conducted by Spiegel, Leproult, & Van Cauter at the University of Chicago has shown that for those who got about four-hours of sleep per night for six nights, hormone function was impaired and a number of bodily functions were degraded. Cortisol levels rose and the body wasn't able to regulate insulin levels. These changes resulted in impaired cognitive functioning and the likelihood of weight gain. The young men who

Avoid bedtime distractions.

volunteered for the sleep-loss study began with blood tests in the normal range and at the end of the one-week study had blood-test results similar to those of diabetics! The good news is that, after resuming healthy sleep patterns for several nights, their blood tests were once again in the normal range.

The amount of sleep needed by adults to function at optimal levels is typically between seven and a half and ten hours per night. Some researchers believe that naps may help you reclaim some lost night-time sleep, but those who research napping (Mednick & Ehrman, 2006) say that naps should typically be less than two hours and you need to be back up again by 5 p.m. or your night-time sleep may be affected.

Scientists at the University of California–San Francisco have evidence that studying until you are tired and then "sleeping on it" improves next day exam performance more than pulling an all-nighter. Improved nerve cell connections during sleep seem to be the reason for this result. These findings are further supported by research showing that information is consolidated while you sleep. So, a good night's sleep actually helps you learn and remember the material you've been studying!

Schedule Time for Friends and Family

Time spent with those we care about is one of life's greatest joys and an investment in future happiness. Since we all have to eat, meals are a wonderful time to connect with family and friends. Having a strong social support network can help motivate you when times are tough. But, like all rewards, make sure the reward helps you meet your goals. Don't use time with your loved ones as an excuse to skip your studies. Those who truly love you want to see you succeed.

What If You Have a Job?

Many students work during college. If you must earn income, excellent time management skills are paramount to your academic success. Each semester carefully calculate the number of hours of personal study required to maintain a strong grade point average. A strong GPA can actually save you money by enabling you to qualify for scholarships, loans and grants. Weigh the benefits of working on campus versus off campus and taking classes full-time versus part-time. Since your course load will change each semester, do not assume your work schedule can always be the same.

Now, let's plan a weekly schedule!

Act & Analyze

Exercise 3

Plan Your Schedule for the Next Week (Plan/Actual)

Use the Plan/Actual Time Recording Sheet on the following page, or use the calendar function on your phone or computer, to plan your schedule for the next week. Schedule in the "Plan" column all your high priority activities such as lecture, labs or small group meetings. Also schedule other necessary activities: job, physical exercise, meals, sleep and R&R. Mark on the "Plan" side when you plan to do your personal study.

You will refer to this schedule several times a day to be sure you are following your plan. You'll feel positively noble as you check off completion of your plan each hour in the "Actual" column. If you did not follow your plan, make a note in the "Actual" column of what you really did with that unit of time. Writing it down will help you identify patterns that may be interfering with your schedule.

At the end of the Plan/Actual Time Recording week, return to this chapter and complete the Check-up for Exercise 3: Plan/Actual Time Recording.

During the week you are completing the Plan/Actual Time Sheet you may continue with this chapter and go on to Step 3, Read and Make Notes.

A full-sized version of the worksheet is available for download from our website: www.VitalStudySkills.com/worksheets

Worksheet 1.2   Plan/Actual Worksheet

Plan your activities for one week. Put a check beside the items you complete at the scheduled time. Write in what you actually did if it was different from your plan. At the end of the week calculate totals for major activities using the following categories: **LEC** (Lecture), **Lab** (Laboratory), **PS** (personal study), **Job, M** (maintenance activities including shopping, cleaning, errands, eating, personal hygiene, etc.), **COM** (commute time), **PE** (physical exercise), **S** (sleep), **R&R** (rest and recreation, including anything that does not fit into previous categories).

	Monday		Tuesday		Wednesday		Thursday		Friday		Saturday		Sunday	
	plan	actual	plan	actual	plan	actual	plan	actual	plan	actual	plan	actual	plan	actual
5:00 a.m.														
6:00														
6:30														
7:00														
7:30														
8:00														
9:00														
10:00														
11:00														
12 noon														
12:30														
1:00														
2:00														
3:00														
4:00														
5:00														
6:00														
6:30														
7:00														
8:00														
9:00														
10:00														
11:00														
12:00														
12:30														
1:00 a.m.														
2:00														
3:00														
4:00														
Daily:														
LEC														
LAB														
Job														
P Study														
COM														
Maint														
P E														
R&R														
Sleep														

Actual weekly totals: Lecture =_____ Lab = _____ Job = _____
Personal Study =_____ Commute = _____ Maintenance =_____
PE =_____ R&R =_____ Sleep =_____

Analyze & Adjust
Check-up for Exercise 3
Plan/Actual Time Recording

Briefly write your answers to the following questions, based on what you have learned from monitoring your time for the past week, using the Plan/Actual Time Recording sheet. Look for patterns.

1. On which days were your planned and actual activities most similar?

   _____

   _____

2. Did you notice a certain time of the day that you were more likely to get off schedule? If yes, describe.

   _____

   _____

3. What did you substitute for planned activities? Can you detect a pattern? For example, did spending too much time in R & R cut down on study time?

   _____

   _____

   _____

4. What changes are needed?

   _____

   _____

5. What was the most helpful idea you learned from this chapter on scheduling your time?

   _____

   _____

If you kept reasonably close to your planned schedule—*Congratulations!*

If your actual time spent was NOT close to what you had planned, you will benefit from another week of Plan/Actual time recording. Revise your plan for the next week, using this experience and analysis, and do a second week of Plan/Actual time recording. At the end of the second week, return to this section and answer the questions above.

It's interesting (and rewarding!) to think about how to accomplish your goals with maximum efficiency. You probably have developed some tricks of your own to save time. Here are some time-saving tips gleaned from busy students who manage to remember friends and family, do all the things they have to do, keep clean and fed and still spend 30-45 hours each week in learning activities.

Things You Can Do To Save Time

1. Do two maintenance or R&R activities at the same time. Note that these are activities that do not typically require a great deal of focused concentration.

   • Listen to music or catch the news or your favorite show while doing maintenance tasks, such as preparing meals, getting dressed or exercising.

   • Sort through flash cards or other notes (see chapter on note making) while waiting for something or someone.

   • Combine social activities with exercise. Walk, jog or go to the gym with a friend.

   • Share a meal with a friend.

2. Many of the "things I have to do" can be accomplished in less time, if you are willing to change.

   • Get a hairstyle that you can fix in a few minutes (really!).

   • Eat food that requires little preparation. Fast food doesn't have to be unhealthy. Fresh vegetables and fruits, served with cheese or nuts, are quick and healthful. Dropping a few nuts in a container of yogurt can be a small meal or a snack. You get the idea.

3. Keep lists for all your regular activities:
   - To avoid extra trips to the store, put items on a "To Buy" list as soon as the need arises. Never go shopping without your list. Bonus: You'll not only save time, you'll also save money if you stick to your list.
   - Keep an errands list and combine as many trips as are practical. Schedule errands on an efficient route to minimize time and mileage. Try not to go out on just one errand at a time.

4. Always carry your calendar with you and refer to it many times a day.

5. Post-it™ notes are great for sticking on a page, phone, computer screen or mirror for temporary reminders that are easily removed after the task is completed.

6. We are not yet a paperless society, so you will probably still have pieces of paper to handle. Create a place to store any bills or statements that you don't have time to deal with immediately. Go through this file every week or two.

7. Be a person who remembers others, even if you are extremely busy. Your phone or a reminder app makes it even easier.

8. Do you ever wander around muttering, "Where did I put my . . . (fill in the blank)?" You can avoid this annoying time-waster by having an assigned place for everything. This applies

especially to small articles that you constantly pick up and put down again, such as keys, phone, glasses or wallets. A visit to a store that sells small, stackable containers may be in order.

9. Try to do things when other people don't. Go to an early movie and eat afterwards. Avoid grocery shopping between 5–6 p.m., or whenever your store is likely to be crowded.

10. Even if you are of legal age, avoid using alcohol or other drugs. That extra drink or two the night before can lead to losing much of the next day. It's hard to pay attention to lectures or studying if you have a headache or are sleepy. Also, remember that alcohol acts as a depressant. Don't drink alcohol before a study session or if you are feeling depressed.

11. Protect study time. Before you begin a study period, decide how you will handle interruptions. If you need to concentrate fully, you will need to minimize interruptions and distractions. See the section on interruptions in Step 5.
    - If a friend begins talking with you while studying, you can say you'd like to have a good visit, pull out your calendar and find convenient time to get together. Or, say you plan to take a short break at a specific time and would enjoy a chat then. Set a timer so you'll remember to get back to work after your visit.
    - If you get a phone call while studying, let the caller leave a message. Better yet, turn the ringer off, to "airplane mode" or "Do Not Disturb" during study periods.
    - Some students pre-empt interruptions by making phone calls between classes, so their social obligations will be taken care of before they begin a study period. Others find they have to turn their phones off and store them in a bag or backpack. Out of sight, out of mind.

12. Do you study with family or friends nearby? Work out a signal that lets them know when you are studying and don't want to be disturbed unless the building is in on fire.

- One student shuts her door and puts up a "Do Not Disturb" sign.
- Many students tell us that mornings, before others are awake, are a good time to study.
- Those with school-aged siblings or children sometimes find that they are able to sit at a large table while they all work on their studies together.
- Other students find that staying on campus for all their study activities works best for them.
- Find at least two good study locations. If one doesn't work out, you'll still have a place to study.

13. Study groups can be helpful or they can be a waste of time. The "50-minute rule" can help you decide if a study group is how you want to spend your valuable study time. Time spent in a study group counts as R&R if more than 10 minutes of any hour is spent off topic. If the group's time is often taken up with talking about a particular instructor, relationships, or lack thereof, then you may want to arrange to meet this group of friends for lunch or a coffee break and spend your precious study time focused on the subject you need to study. Arum & Roska, 2011, found that it is typically more useful to study alone than in a group.

   Better yet, form a Quiz Group of three to five students that meets at least 24 to 48 hours in advance of an exam. Students who belong to effective small groups, tell us that the participants have agreed to spend time outside the group studying and learning the material and then come together to review and test each other on it.

14. A digital timer is a great study tool. Using a timer can help you keep track of both study periods and break times. Using a timer is a good way to figure out how long things actually take and can also help keep you on task. They are inexpensive and useful in many situations. You can also use your phone for this, but as one student told us, "No one can call or text me on my timer!"

Let's Talk about Procrastination

If there were no benefits to procrastination, no one would do it. People who are life-long procrastinators tell us:

> Procrastination gives you a rush when you are able to complete the project just minutes (or seconds) ahead of the deadline.

> Procrastination gives you a built-in excuse for failure. "Oh, I put it off too long. If I had started earlier, I would have done better."

> Procrastinators sometimes feel they are "getting away with" something by waiting until the last possible moment to begin a project.

But, as you can imagine, there are also downsides to procrastination.

> Procrastination does not allow you to do your best work. There is no time for reflection or fine-tuning.

> Procrastination creates anxiety, which may cause you to avoid the task at hand. (Which in turn creates more stress and anxiety as you fall further behind!)

> Procrastination sets up a cycle of wasting time and then trying to reclaim that time all at once.

> Procrastination does not allow for the inevitable reality of delays, mistakes and illnesses that occur in everyone's life.

If you examine the two lists above, you will notice that the first list, of so-called benefits of procrastination, involves fleeting emotions. Achieving excellence is not part of the procrastination pay-off. If you are a chronic postponer, you know there are other feelings that also go along with procrastinating, such as guilt, fear, dread, worry, anxiety and sometimes anger. Procrastination is like gambling with time. You get an initial rush from the risk, but the long-term effect is harmful. Odds are, sooner or later, some unexpected event will derail you.

The good news is that behavioral experts tell us that procrastination is just a bad habit and can be remedied like any other habit you would like to replace. First, by becoming aware of the habit or pattern and then, by taking the steps necessary to remedy it. Once you begin to reap the rewards of having a steady study schedule, it is unlikely that you will want to return to the anxiety-ridden days of procrastinating!

For those who protest that they "do their best work under pressure," you can create your own "pressure" which will not have the disastrous consequences of missing a deadline. For example, if the professor says your 20-page paper on "Causes of the Civil War" is due on a Tuesday morning, you could set your deadline to finish the paper on the Friday evening prior to that date. If you mark it in your calendar and tell yourself, your friends and maybe a trusted advisor, it MUST be finished by that date, then you can still enjoy the thrill of working under pressure, while also building in a day or two to review and improve your paper. If you take the time to analyze and revise your work, you are also likely to receive a higher grade, which should also help reinforce your new habit of setting an earlier deadline. For additional ideas on how to deal with procrastination see the books by Fiore or Knaus or the website maintained by Pychyl, all of which are listed in the references at the end of this chapter.

One final consideration about procrastination—examine your study area. Is it messy, cluttered or uninviting in some way? If so, this could be one of the reasons you don't like to use that space. Look at Step 5 for ideas on how to arrange your study area so you can get the maximum benefit from your study time. You'll be amazed at how a properly equipped study space can boost your efficiency!

Tip: If you have gotten yourself into a hole, by falling behind in a class, and must dig your way out, here is a suggestion. This is only a stop-gap measure to be used in an emergency. If you are behind in a class, it is usually better to start by catching up with the most current information and add in the older, missed information along the way. Don't get further behind by trying to catch up from the beginning while the class gets further and further ahead.

Analyze & Adjust
What Have You Learned?

1. What was the main thing you learned from working your way through this chapter on time management?

   _____

   _____

   _____

2. What is one thing you can change to become a better time manager?

   _____

   _____

   _____

3. Interviews with writers, poets, painters and others who are considered "creative types" (see *Daily Rituals: How Artists Work,* by Mason Currey) reveal that many of them lead very structured lives. How might having a regular routine contribute to the creative process?

   _____

   _____

   _____

⟫ Summary

Your time is valuable—not just the big chunks of weeks, months and years, but the small bits of minutes and hours. Use your time well and you will reap the rewards!

Some students find themselves in the challenging position of having to juggle school, family and employment. There will be a period of adjustment as you learn to prioritize and set boundaries. The more quickly you learn to do that—to figure out what needs to be done and then act on it—the shorter your period of adjustment will be. But the only way to know how your time is spent is to measure your time, which is why we created the Baseline and Plan/Actual Time recording sheets for you to use.

If you are a person whose full time job is being a student—then consider yourself fortunate. Give your studies the attention they deserve in order for you to succeed.

The exercises in this chapter have been designed to help you clearly understand how you spend your time and learn how to plan a schedule that will allow you to achieve your goals as a college student. It takes time to get where you want to go. You can develop a good learning system only if you schedule enough time for the work.

A bonus for excellent time scheduling is the feeling of confidence in knowing that you have designed your life to have enough time for all your responsibilities and your pleasures!

》》 References

Allen, D. (2002). *Getting things done: The art of stress-free productivity.* New York: Penguin Books.

To be productive you must be able to think clearly. To think clearly, you need to be able to "download" your short-term memory or "to-do lists." This will allow the mind to do what it does best—process information.

Arum, R. and Roska, J. (2011). *Academically adrift: Limited learning on college campuses.* Chicago: University of Chicago Press.

Page 98 cites the ineffectiveness of study groups compared with time spent in personal study.

Association for Psychological Science (2010, December 17). Sleep makes your memories stronger, and helps with creativity. *Science Daily.* http://www.sciencedaily.com/releases/2010/11/101113165441.htm

"The [sleeping] brain is busy. It's not just consolidating memories; it's organizing them and picking out the most salient information."

Buzsâki, György. (1998). Memory consolidation during sleep: A neurophysiological perspective. *Journal of Sleep Research.* Vol. 7, Supplement 1, 17–23. http://onlinelibrary.wiley.com/doi/10.1046/j.1365-2869.7.s1.3.x/pdf

"Transfer of the stored representations to neocortical areas is carried by . . . neuronal bursts (called sharp wave bursts) initiated in the hippocampus during slow wave sleep."

Curry, M. (2013). *Daily rituals: How artists work.* New York: Knopf.

The author reviewed the routines from an array of interviews, diaries, letters, and magazine profiles to discover more about their daily lives and schedules.

Fiore, N. (2007). *The now habit: A strategic program for overcoming procrastination and enjoying guilt-free play.* NY: Tarcher/Putnam.

The author has developed the "un-schedule" to help overcome procrastination by scheduling fun and social activities first.

Gupta, S. (March 13, 2006). Your time: Sleep deprived. *Time Magazine,* p. 68.

Dr. Gupta reports on his personal experience of a sleep deprivation experiment.

Howard, P.J. (2nd edition 2000). *The owner's manual for the brain: everyday applications from mind-brain research.* Atlanta: Bard Press.

Chapter 7 is entitled A Good Night's Sleep: Cycles, Dreams, Naps and Nightmares and reviews research of each, including the link between sleep and memory and how to promote regular sleeping habits.

Jaggars, S.S. (2014). Choosing between online and face-to-face courses: Community college student voices. *American Journal of Distance Education,* Volume 28, Issue 1.
http://ccrc.tc.columbia.edu/media/k2/attachments/online-demand-student-voices.pdf

Jenkins, R. (2012, March 13). Online classes and college completion. *The Chronicle of Higher Education.*

Kabat-Zinn, J. (2003). Mindfulness-based interventions in context: Past, present, and future. *Clinical Psychology: Science and Practice.* Vol.10, No. 2, 144–156.
DOI: 10.1093/clipsy/bpg016
http://www-psych.stanford.edu/~pgoldin/Buddhism/MBSR2003_Kabat-Zinn.pdf

"Mindfulness can be defined as paying attention to one's inner and outer experiences in a non-judgmental manner from moment to moment."

Kitsantas, A., Winsler, A., & Huie, F. (2008). Self-regulation and ability predictors of academic success during college: A predictive validity study. *Journal of Advanced Academics,* 20, 42–68.

Time management skills and learning strategies contribute to successful academic outcomes.

Knaus, W.J. (1997). *Do it now!: Break the procrastination habit.* Hoboken, N.J.: Wiley.

Using the "awareness/action" approach, Knaus shows readers how to identify root causes for procrastination and suggests solutions. One of his more widely known methods is the "five minute rule" where you promise yourself to work for only five minutes on a task you'd prefer to avoid—and then after the first five minutes decide whether to continue or to quit. Most people find they will continue working past the five minute mark.

Mednick, S.C., & Ehrman, M. (2006). *Take a nap! Change your life.* New York: Workman Publishing.

This book discusses the research on the benefits of napping and shows you how to plan the optimum nap to increase alertness, strengthen memory and reduce stress.

Pauk, W. (1997). *How to study in college*. Boston: Houghton Mifflin Company.

Study skills book for college students that includes a section on procrastination.

Pychyl, T. (2014). Procrastination Research Group (PRG), Carleton University, Ottawa, Canada, Department of Psychology. Retrieved from http://http-server.carleton.ca/~tpychyl/

The website noted above originates at Carleton University, but represents a compilation of information and research on procrastination from all over the world.

Rosen, L.D., Lim, A.F., Carrier, L.M., & Cheever, N.A. (2011). An empirical examination of the educational impact of text message-induced task switching in the classroom: Educational implications and strategies to enhance learning, *Psicologia Educativa, 17*(2), 163–177. http://my.psychologytoday.com/files/attachments/40095/anempiricalexaminationoftheeducationalimpactoftextmessage-inducedtaskswitchingintheclassroom-educati.pdf

This study examines the effect of sending and receiving text messages on classroom learning. Results found that the High Texting group scored significantly worse (10.6% lower) than the No/Low Texting Interruption group.

Rossi, E.L. (1991). *The twenty minute break: Reduce stress, maximize performance, improve health and emotional well-being using the new science of ultradian rhythms*. LA: Tarcher.

Ultradian rhythms are the natural biological rhythms that occur more than once a day. According to Rossi, our mind and body systems benefit from a period of about 20 minutes' rest every 1½ to 2 hours.

Schwarz, T., Gomes, J. and McCarthy C. (2010). *The way we're working isn't working: The four forgotten needs that energize great performance*. NY: Free Press. Re-titled (2011) as: *Be excellent at anything: The four keys to transforming the way we work and live*.

This book offers simple and powerful tips on how to build your ability to better deal with the demands we face every day.

Science Codex. Link between sleep loss and psychiatric disorders. http://www.sciencecodex.com/study_provides_first_evidence_of_neural_link_between_sleep_loss_and_psychiatric_disorders

This article shows evidence between sleep loss and psychiatric disorders. Some form of sleep disruption appears to be present in almost all psychiatric disorders.

Spiegel K, Leproult R, Tasali E, Penev P, & Van Cauter E. (2004). Sleep curtailment results in decreased leptin levels, elevated ghrelin levels and increased hunger and appetite. *Annals Int Med*, 141 (11):846–850.

Lack of adequate sleep appears to influence hormones that regulate the feeling of fullness (leptin) and hunger (ghrelin) in a way that could stimulate over-eating.

Spiegel, K., Leproult, R., & Van Cauter, E. (1999). Impact of a sleep debt on metabolic and endocrine function. *The Lancet*, 354, 1435–1439.

Rise in cortisol, also known as the "stress hormone," and slowing of glucose metabolism occur with lack of sleep, even over a short period of time. Elevated cortisol levels have been linked with memory impairment.

Stickgold, R. & Walker, M. (2007). Sleep-dependent memory consolidation and reconsolidation. *Sleep Medicine*. Vol. 8, 331–343. http://walkerlab.berkeley.edu/reprints/Stickgold&Walker_Sleep%20Medicine_2007.pdf

The process of memory consolidation is a continuing series of biological adjustments that enhance the efficiency and usefulness of stored memories over time.

Time Tracking Forms. Study Guides and Strategies Website.

Daily schedule: http://www.studygs.net/schedule/
Weekly schedule: http://www.studygs.net/schedule/weekly.htm

U.S. Department of Education. (March 18, 2011). Office of Postsecondary Education. http://ifap.ed.gov/dpcletters/attachments/GEN1106.pdf

Guidance to institutions and accrediting agencies regarding a credit hour as defined in the final regulations published on October 29, 2010.

Van Cauter, E., Leproult, R. & Plat, L. (2000). Age-related changes in slow wave sleep and REM sleep and relationship with growth hormone and cortisol levels in healthy men. *Journal of the American Medical Association,* 284, 861–868.

A rise in cortisol, also known as the "stress hormone," and slowing of glucose metabolism occur with lack of sleep, even over a short period of time. Elevated cortisol levels have been linked with memory impairment.

van der Helm E., Gujar N., Walker M.P. (2010). Sleep deprivation impairs the accurate recognition of human emotions. *SLEEP.* 33(3):335–342.
http://www.journalsleep.org/viewabstract.aspx?pid=27729

This study investigated the impact of being sleep deprived on a person's ability to recognize the intensity of another person's facial emotions.

Vital Study Skills. Our website has downloadable forms for you to use. www.VitalStudySkills.com/worksheets

STEP **TWO**
Prepare to Get More Out of Lecture and Reading (Pre-read)

(WEEK 2)

QUIZ Preparing for Lecture

Directions: Mark the number that most accurately describes your behavior.

Yes / True	Sometimes	No / False	
0	1	2	**1.** Before a lecture I read the book, handouts or PowerPoint® slides to see what information will be covered.
0	1	2	**2.** I know what the main ideas of the lecture topic will be before the lecture begins.
0	1	2	**3.** I can usually correctly spell the key words used in lecture.
0	1	2	**4.** I can quickly (10–15 minutes) go through a chapter in a book and pick out the important points.

Yes / True	Sometimes	No / False		
0	1	2	**5.**	Even before a lecture begins, I have an idea of what form my lecture notes will take (e.g., diagrams, charts, flash cards, loose notes.)
2	1	0	**6.**	I am often sleepy during lecture.
2	1	0	**7.**	I spend too much time reworking and rewriting my notes after a lecture.
2	1	0	**8.**	It's hard for me to understand what the lecturer is talking about.
2	1	0	**9.**	I have difficulty concentrating during lecture.
2	1	0	**10.**	There are always a lot of new, unfamiliar vocabulary words used in lecture.
_____				**Total Score** (Add the numbers circled.)

FEEDBACK on Preparing for Lecture

1. Since about one-third to one-half of your study time is spent in lecture, why not make it as efficient as possible? Looking ahead at what will be covered in class is an excellent way to improve your understanding and retention of the lecture and reading assignments.

2. You'll feel smart knowing what is coming next. Being able to anticipate is an important part of critical thinking. You will also be able to ask intelligent questions in class.

3. Making notes is a lot easier if you are already familiar with the vocabulary.

4. The ability to pick out the main ideas and related details is another facet of critical thinking. The point of pre-reading is to RAPIDLY determine the big picture. If you're spending more than 10–15 minutes, you're reading the text. Reading the text is obviously important, but pre-reading BEFORE reading is the key to increasing comprehension, retention and reading speed.

5. Making condensed notes either before or during class is a real time saver!

6. Feeling sleepy can have many causes, the chief one being lack of sleep. Not being mentally engaged or challenged can also be a cause. If you are already familiar with a topic, it will be more interesting. Also, if you have a general idea where the lecturer is going, you will be able to capture the important details in your notes. You're less likely to feel sleepy when you are actively involved in note-making during class.

7. On average, about half of your study time may be spent making your highly organized study notes. If that sounds like a lot of time, remember it is the process of organizing the information that helps you build mental models of what you are learning.

8. Knowing the key topics in advance allows you to put the bits and pieces of a rambling lecture into the right format. Having some knowledge beforehand will help you ask better questions.

9. You will not get lost during lecture if you have an idea of where the lecture is going. Being engaged in the topic and discussion will help you concentrate.

10. If you have pre-read, the vocabulary will be familiar. Since you won't have to stop and ponder "what does that mean?," you'll get more out of lecture and have a better set of notes.

A score of 0–5 is very good. **Great job!**

A score between 6–9 means you could get more out of lecture with additional preparation.

A score of 10–20 means you could definitely make better use of lecture by pre-reading. Give it a try!

❱❱ Why Prepare for Lecture?

Preparing for lecture will increase your understanding of the information presented in class. It will also increase your reading speed and comprehension and help you make notes more rapidly. If you are not currently pre-reading, you may think of it as an "extra step." It's not. We are teaching you a system that is both effective *and* efficient. Pre-reading will actually save you time. You'll have an opportunity to try it for yourself in just a few minutes.

How to Get the Most of Out of Lecture

Many students don't know how to make the best use of lecture time. You have surely noticed classmates who are asleep, half-asleep, texting, checking emails or just daydreaming.

One student said, "I like to pretend I'm live-Tweeting the lecture as I make my notes in class. That way I have to think about what the more important or interesting parts are."

Though lectures (either live or recorded) may not be the most efficient method for conveying information, they do offer some advantages.

Benefits of Attending Lecture (Live or Recorded)

1. Gives you an idea of what the instructor thinks is important (and therefore likely to be on the test)
2. Imposes order on the information (from the handouts and/or the lecture itself)

3. Provides an auditory mode of input (hearing it)
4. Often adds the most recent information that has not yet made it to the text books
5. Presents an opportunity to ask questions about something that is unclear to you and to hear the questions of other students
6. Gives you an opportunity to get to know your professors (and for them to know you).

If you are familiar with the material *before* lecture, it is much easier to pick out the patterns that emerge from the information. Structuring the information according to these patterns is a very important step in the learning process, as you will learn in Step 3 on note-making.

How often a topic is mentioned is an indicator of its importance and its likelihood of appearing on a test. Anything that is mentioned in multiple resources, you can typically count on seeing again—on an exam. Whatever form your notes take (we'll discuss note types in the next chapter), the more important concepts and details need to be featured prominently.

Close attention will help you figure out what is important to each of your lecturers. Instructors tell us that they typically cover in lecture 60–70% of what they plan to ask on the exam. The rest of the information is from assigned or "recommended" resources.

"Reading" Your Instructor

If you are able to observe your professor while he or she teaches, here are some tips that may help you learn to "read" your instructors:

> If they want to make sure you are reading the text, sometimes teachers will purposefully not mention something in lecture but will direct you to the assigned reading material.

> Lecturers will sometimes mention a general topic during lecture or on a handout and then, when writing the exam questions, will ask a specific detail about that topic which is found only in the text or other reference materials.

> After the instructors and/or course director go to all the trouble of creating the course objectives, they are very likely to return to them for test items.

> The number of times a concept or topic is mentioned will help you gauge its importance to the lecturer.

> Physical cues include:

  • use of voice (loud, soft, pauses)
  • pointing
  • writing or tapping on board
  • saying, "Take home point," "This is important," "Do you understand this?"
  • telling a story.

What other cues have you seen your instructors use?

Pre-reading Is the Key to Getting the Most Out of Lecture

While preparing for lecture can certainly consist of *more* than pre-reading, we believe that pre-reading is the *least* you should do before attending a lecture. Pre-reading will help activate your prior knowledge. That means it will help you remember what you already know about the topic. If the topic is new to you, it will help you begin building a solid foundation for your learning and understanding of the topic.

When you return to read the text more thoroughly after pre-reading, you will increase both your reading speed and your comprehension. Talk about efficient!

What Is Pre-reading?

> **Skimming and Scanning.** If it takes more than 10–15 minutes to pre-read, you're not pre-reading, you are reading. You'll know the difference between reading and pre-reading by how much time it takes. Fast, fast, fast!

> Looking for the **main idea(s).** What is the big picture or the main point of the section or chapter?

You're not really prepared for class until you have pre-read.

> Looking at the **illustrations and diagrams** (and the text below them). The bigger and more colorful the pictures are, the more important the topic is likely to be.

> Learning the **vocabulary, new terms or abbreviations** that will be used in the lecture. You can highlight them or, better yet, make flash cards.

> **Discovering patterns.** Look for relationships. How do the subtopics relate to the main concept? How many important details do there seem to be? Are there numbered lists with details about each item? Compare and contrast? Look for clusters of information. There will be more about this in the next chapter.

> What kind of information is it? **Analyze** whether the information is cause and effect, the steps in a process, a diagram with structures to remember, etc. Step 3 will give more detailed explanation about this type of analysis.

How a textbook is arranged will give you clues as to what is important. For example, lots of space and lots of color means that the author and/or publisher think the topic is important.

Getting Acquainted with Your Textbook (e-book or print)

Since you will be spending at least the next semester with your textbooks, why not get to know them and learn what they have to offer?

Take a minute and get out one of your printed textbooks—or open an e-book. Look through the table of contents. That is the *Very Big Picture*. Are there any interesting looking entries? Turn to the back of the book. Is there an index? What type of information is listed there? Are there any appendices? What is included in those? Have you visited the publisher's website? Does the site have chapter outlines or sample test questions? Now that you know these are available, you will be prepared to use them.

Each textbook is designed to have a different approach to the information and will often include study aids. Start with the publisher's website associated with your book. The website has clues as to what the publisher thinks is important for you to know. If you are using an e-book, click on the various links and see what resources are offered. This exercise can be a real time-saver later on. If your instructors refer to that study aid, you'll already know what they are referring to and where to find it. Once you are familiar with the tools and resources offered, you will be able to quickly tell when (and whether) to use each one. For example, are the practice questions too easy? If so, skip them and find another resource that asks higher level or more difficult questions. (Note: teachers may assume you haven't visited the resource section and may draw exam questions from them.)

Some of you may be thinking, "If a little bit is good, then more is even better!" Hold on. Do NOT attempt to use every study aid or resource for every course! Find out what resources are available and then choose the one or two that are most useful for that particular course. Using too many resources will lead to feeling overwhelmed by the abundance of information. Evaluate the resources offered, and then choose only one or two.

Sources for Pre-reading
You may pre-read from a variety of materials:

> Course textbooks

> Course syllabus

> PowerPoint® slides or other handouts

> Review books

> Online resources (e.g., Wikipedia, YouTube, Khan Academy, etc.)

Remember: You can't pre-read from every source available, so you'll need to choose the best one (or two) for each class. Be prepared to find new resources for each class offered.

What to Look for When You Pre-read

> Study questions—read these first (they will point to what the authors think is the most important information),

> Summary—read this next (brief overview of the whole chapter).

Then quickly flip (or scroll) through the pages in a chapter and look for:

> Main headings

> Bold-faced print

> Boxed information

> Diagrams and pictures

> Charts, tables and graphs.

When you pre-read you are interacting with the text, instead of being a passive bystander. Do you already know something about the topic? See if you can connect new information to something you already know. This type of active engagement helps you remember information longer.

Sometimes you will not be given much (or any) information about an upcoming lecture except the topic. Don't despair! The internet will come in handy here. Look at Wikipedia or YouTube to find a quick introduction or overview. While many faculty members may not allow you to use these resources for scholarly

papers, they are often a good starting place for an introduction to a topic. Online resources with animations are especially useful when learning a process, cycle, sequence or anything that changes over time. Watching an animation may give you the "aha!" that was missing from reading and looking at diagrams.

Critical Thinking Is Part of Pre-reading and Active Learning

Critical thinking includes asking questions as you read, such as:

> What do I already know about this topic?

> What is the main point? (Can I say it more simply?)

> How are the details related to the main point?

> What patterns can I detect?

When to Pre-read

If your classes are scheduled back-to-back, it may be difficult to pre-read immediately before a lecture. So when can you pre-read? The best time is often the evening before the next day's lectures. Other options are to get up fifteen minutes earlier in the morning or pre-read during your lunch break for that day's classes. Find the time that works best for you each semester and then stick with it. These few minutes of preparation will very quickly pay big dividends!

Work on increasing your vocabulary as you pre-read. Keep a stack of blank note cards or sheet of paper at hand. You can quickly jot down unfamiliar words as you see them and write out the definitions either while you pre-read or before lecture. If you have the discipline to use your computer or phone while pre-reading, you can create electronic flashcards instead. Some resources include: Quizlet, StudyBlue, FlashcardMachine, ANKI and many others. These sites (and your textbook's) may have pre-made flashcards, or you may make your own. Ask those who've taken the class recently what the best resources are—then evaluate your options and decide for yourself. Just because it worked for someone else, doesn't mean it's the best resource for you.

Why do all that work? Increasing your vocabulary will help you on every standardized exam you take for the rest of your life. If you learn a few new words each day or week while you're in college—and not just in your major field of study—you will have a wide vocabulary by the time you graduate. You'll be glad you did.

Preparing for Online Courses

Preparing for online courses will be very similar to preparing for a regular class, though your resources may differ. Perhaps your instructor will ask you to watch a video in preparation for a class instead of reading a chapter. The same guidelines apply, however; the more you do before class, the more you will get out of class and the less you will have to do afterwards.

Act & Analyze

Exercise 1

Pre-reading Trial Run

Choose a chapter from any book that will be covered in lecture in the next few days (preferably tomorrow). Set a timer for 10 minutes to pre-read the section you've chosen. Count the number of pages before you begin, so you'll know how to pace yourself. Return to Check-Up for Exercise 1, below, when you've finished.

Guidelines for the Pre-reading Exercise

> Set a timer for 10 minutes.

> Give yourself a positive purpose for reading and a reason to remember what you've read. The objectives in your course syllabus will be a good guide here.

> Look for the general concepts, not the details.

> Look for cues that indicate most important ideas and terms (use of color, headlines, indentations, charts, italics, bold, illustrations, diagrams, figures).

> Move your eyes down the page quickly. You should feel a slight tension about getting through this material in the time you've allowed.

> Go!

Analyze

Check-Up for Exercise 1
Pre-reading Trial Run

1. What were the main points or topics in the chapter or section you pre-read?

   _____

   _____

2. If there were several points or topics, how do they relate to each other?

   _____

   _____

   _____

3. Do you remember any of the details? How do they relate to the main point?

_____

_____

_____

_____

4. Were there any large or colorful graphics? If yes, what were they about?

_____

_____

_____

_____

Even though most students do not currently prepare by pre-reading before class, studies (and common sense) have shown that pre-reading will increase your understanding and help you remember the information for a longer period of time. By pre-reading you can figure out what you already know about the topic, what is important, get better lecture notes and recall information more easily on tests.

Some students find it helpful to think of pre-reading as watching a movie preview. The preview shows you who the main characters are, a little bit about the story line and the type of movie it is (action, comedy, tear-jerker, etc.). It helps set your expectations for what the movie will be about.

Act
Exercise 2
Incorporate Pre-reading in Your Schedule

Your assignment for this week is to pre-read for at least one of your more difficult classes each day. You can either pre-read for morning lectures the previous night, or get up a bit earlier and pre-read that morning. You may want to pre-read for afternoon classes during your lunch break. The idea is to have the information fresh in your brain when you attend (or listen to) the lecture.

Complete the exercise below after you have pre-read for one week.

Analyze & Adjust
Check-Up for Exercise 2
Incorporate Pre-reading in Your Schedule

How did pre-reading affect your lecture experience?

_____

_____

_____

_____

You'll be pleasantly surprised how much more you get out of lecture when you are prepared!

)) Summary

Pre-reading is the second step in our six-step study system. Students who pre-read:

> Save time

> Learn more from lecture

> Actively participate in class discussions

> Read the text faster

> Make notes more quickly

> Remember information longer

> Feel smart.

)) References

Ausubel, D. P. (1960). The use of advance organizers in the learning and retention of meaningful verbal material. *Journal of Educational Psychology,* 51(5), 267–272.

Ausubel, D. P. (2000). *The acquisition and retention of knowledge: A cognitive view.* Boston: Kluwer Academic Publishers.

Cook, L.K., & Mayer, R.E. (1988). Teaching readers about the structure of a scientific text. *Journal of Educational Psychology,* 80, 448–456.

College biology students showed substantial gains in recall of high conceptual information when they had previously noted the organization of information presented in the text: enumeration, sequence, or comparison and contrast.

Gurlitt, J. Dummel, S. Schuster, S.; Nückles, M. (2012, March). Differently structured advance organizers lead to different initial schemata and learning outcomes. *Instructional Science* vol. 40 issue 2. p. 351–369. http://lsc.ecnu.edu.cn/images/2012/1989/Differently%20 structured%20advance%20organizers%20lead%20to%20 different%20initial%20schemata%20and%20learning%20 outcomes.pdf

Jacobowitz, T. (1981). The effects of modified skimming on college students' recall and recognition of expository text. *Directions in Reading: Research and Instruction.* The National Reading Conference, Inc., Washington, D.C., pp. 232–237.

Advance knowledge of the text facilitates understanding. Skimming provides insight into the text by exposing the reader to many of the major points intended by the author.

Karlin, R. (1969). *Reading for achievement.* New York: Holt, Rinehart, Winston, Inc.

Provides detailed instructions on pages 3–25 on how to pre-read.

Kitsantas, A., Winsler, A., & Huie, F. (2008). Self-regulation and ability predictors of academic success during college: A predictive validity study. *Journal of Advanced Academics,* 20, 42–68.

Good time management skills and learning strategies contribute to successful academic outcomes.

Krug, D., George, B., Hannon, S.A., & Glover, J.A. (1989). The effect of outlines and headings on readers' recall of text. *Contemporary Educational Psychology,* 14 (2), 111–123.

Students who read outlines prior to reading the texts recall information better on later tests.

Redding, R.E. (1990). Metacognitive instruction: Trainers teaching thinking skills. *Performance Improvement Quarterly,* 3 (1), 27–41.

Review of research in critical thinking skills.

Snapp, J.C., & Glover J.A. (1990). Advance organizers and study questions. *Journal of Educational Research,* 83 (51), 266–271.

Students who pre-read the text, or had an overview, gave significantly better answers to higher order study questions.

Spencer, F., Johnston, M., & Ames, W. (1981). The effect of manipulating the advance organizer and other pre-reading strategies on comprehension of abstract text. *Directions in Reading: Research and Instruction.* The National Reading Conference, Inc., Washington, D.C., pp. 228–231.

Pre-reading can significantly increase the processing of unfamiliar or abstract material, especially if the material is not well organized.

Tudor, I. (1986). Advance organisers as adjuncts to reading comprehension. *Journal of Research in Reading*, 9 (2), 103–115.

Experiment showed advance organizers facilitate comprehension especially for more complex texts. The greater the level of textual difficulty, the more benefit advance organizers provide.

Wade, S.E., Reynolds, R.E. (1989). Developing metacognitive awareness. *Journal of Reading*, 33 (1), 6–14.

Deciding what to study, or "what is important," is a key component to skillful reading. Skilled learners pay extra attention to main ideas of the text and are aware of textual clues that point to key ideas. The clues are headings, topic sentences, amount of space author gives to the idea, bold-face type, italics, lists and study questions provided.

Winne, P. H., & Hadwin, A. F. (1998). *Studying as self-regulated learning. Metacognition in educational theory and practice.* Hillsdale: Erlbaum.
http://www4.ncsu.edu/~jlnietfe/Metacog_Articles_files/Winne%20%26%20Hadwin%20(1998).pdf

Describes the COPES model which includes: conditions, operations, products, evaluations, standards. These are the steps that students use in the process of studying.

Read and Make Notes

(WEEK 3)

QUIZ Note-Making

Directions: Mark the number that best describes your actual study behavior.

Yes / True	Sometimes	No / False	
2	1	0	**1.** I highlight important information, sometimes more than a third of each page.
0	1	2	**2.** Within a day of lecture I rewrite or reorganize my notes.
2	1	0	**3.** I don't understand a lot of what I read.
0	1	2	**4.** I keep paper and pencil or my computer handy and make notes while I read.
0	1	2	**5.** I put my notes into a condensed format (cards, charts, diagram or outlines) for later review.
0	1	2	**6.** My notes show how the details are related to the main ideas.
0	1	2	**7.** My notes are in a format designed for quick and easy review.

Yes / True	Sometimes	No / False	
0	1	2	**8.** When my self-testing shows that I don't remember an important detail, I put that detail on a flash card and review until I have learned it.
2	1	0	**9.** I often forget the big picture and get lost in the details.
0	1	2	**10.** I use visual cues (color or white space) to make relationships stand out in my notes.

_____ **Total Score** (Add up all the circled answers to get your total score.)

FEEDBACK on Note-Making

1. Books highlighted in many colors may look pretty but aren't very useful. Highlighting is okay for marking main ideas, some of the important details or vocabulary words but can't be used efficiently for review or self-test. If a lot of the text is highlighted or underlined, there will be too much material to review. Also, highlighting does not help put details in the context of main ideas. Authors of textbooks usually already have highlighted the main topics and details by using larger font size, bolded text and colors.

2. Rewriting and organizing your notes within a day or two of the lecture ensures that you will always be caught up and will not have to cram before an exam. It is best to make your notes while the information from the lecture and reading is still fresh and vivid in your mind.

3. If you're thinking "I don't understand this" as you read, you need to go through the process of making very organized

notes in order to see the relationships among the details presented. You are probably just getting lost in how the details relate to the main idea—or to each other. But if there really is a complex concept to conquer see the section called, "What to Do When You Don't Understand" later in this chapter.

4. The goal of note-making is to eliminate having to refer to the textbook itself. We want you to get the information into a highly organized, compact form that you can review repeatedly and use for self-testing. Making notes on a separate sheet of paper or your computer as you read your books is the first step toward creating an excellent set of notes.

5. Condensing your notes into outlines, tables, charts, diagrams, or cards calls for analysis of the nature of the information to be learned. Is the information a list of things to remember? Does it consist of main topics with a series of sub-topics that are similar in some way? Does the information occur in a sequence? Is it primarily visual, like a diagram? This analysis is the big picture. Experts on learning call it *metacognition*, which is the ability to assess your own level of knowledge. Research shows that metacognition and contextual organization are keys to understanding and recall.

6. Many students have told us that learning to make a set of highly-organized, condensed notes was the most useful study skill they ever acquired (after learning to spend enough time studying). Why? Because it forced them to think about the structure of the information to be learned and it made reviewing and self-testing easy.

7. Repetition. Repetition. Repetition. It can't be said too often. Repetition is the key to memory. Make it your motto. If you create condensed notes in a format that you can review easily, you will be able to review your notes more often.

8. The beauty of flash cards is their portability - paper ones fit easily into your bag or pocket and electronic versions are on your phone. They are easy to review, even in odd bits of time, such as waiting for class to begin or during a break. As you go through your set of cards, you can sort them into those which you "know" and "don't know." The sorting allows you to continually spend your time on what you *don't* know. Reviewing them often (5–10 times) during the day will help you remember important details that self-testing showed you do not yet recall easily.

9. Losing track of the big picture will not happen once you acquire the habit of making good study notes. Good notes relate the details to the main ideas. Getting lost in the details usually means you are trying to learn them out of the context of the bigger picture.

10. You want to be able to review your notes quickly so you can go over them repeatedly in the time available. Visual aids (use of color, boxes) allow you to get your eyes over your notes rapidly. We've found that many of our students actually enjoy and take pride in making their notes, because they are interesting and colorful.

SCORE INTERPRETATION   Note-Making
0–5 = Very good!
6–10 = Good but could use improvement
11–20 = This chapter can really, really help you!

No matter what your score you will definitely learn something useful in this chapter. Good note makers can become GREAT note makers! We'll show you how to organize your notes so the details are easy to remember.

⟫ How to Choose the Best Note Format

You are about to learn the most effective way to create notes for ease in studying and recalling lots of detailed information. We will also show you how to choose the best note-making format.

This chapter will present specific research-based methods on how to create your own notes to help you more easily understand information and store the information in your long-term memory.

Computer Use for Class Notes

Many students take their laptop or tablet to class and try to capture information during lecture. But those same students tell us that they really aren't able to pay attention to what the instructor is saying while busily trying to format and input everything that is said. So it's important to have a plan for how you will capture information in each class.

For example, if your teacher sends out the slides he plans to use in class, you can make your own notes in the notes section of each slide or use an app that allows you to make notes on the slides. You could create a template while pre-reading for class and use that template to make notes during class, or simply annotate handouts during class and create your own notes after class. The secret is to create a strategy that works best for each class.

Distractions and Multitasking The research is very clear. While many people think they are able to multi-task well, they aren't. In fact, those considered "heavy media users" are actually worse at switching tasks than "light media users" (Ophir, Nass & Wagner, 2009) and even those not using computers during class can be distracted by those who are (Sana, Weston, Cepeda, 2013)!

No one can do two tasks simultaneously and well, if they both require your full attention. At best, you are switching between tasks about once a second. That doesn't sound too bad until you add in the fact that a distraction that catches your full attention will impede your ability to easily go back to the other task. For example, if you get a text during class that says, "Meet for lunch?" it might not be very distracting if it's from your best friend. But if you receive that same text from the cute guy or girl you've wanted to go out with, it might be a bit more distracting.

Step 5 will have more suggestions about how to deal with distractions and interruptions, but the bottom line is: minimizing distractions—or potential distractions—will increase focus, which will increase what you remember. Classes that are more challenging will require a higher level of concentration.

Paper and Pen(cil)   The other option for making notes during class is to use the plain old pen (or pencil) and paper method. The process of actually writing things down by hand has kinesthetic benefits that you don't experience when using a keyboard. But writing things by hand often takes longer, so keep that in mind when deciding which method to use. You may need to experiment with both (or other) methods to see what works best for you in a particular class. Just because everyone else is taking notes in a certain way does not mean that is the best way for *you* to make notes. Each method has pros and cons and different classes will require different methods of note making.

Research reported in *Science Daily* (2009) indicates that "doodling" while listening can help you focus and retain information better, so there's another reason to use paper!

If you are preparing by pre-reading before you go to class, you will already have a good idea of where the lecture will go, and if it will be possible to make fairly complete notes during class. Reading the text later will help you fill in details before you make your final set of notes—either on the computer or by hand.

What to Include in Your Study Notes

How will you choose what to put in your notes? You will be drawing from a variety of sources, primarily:

> Required book(s)

> Course syllabus and objectives

> Instructor handouts/downloads

> Lectures

> Supplemental resources (articles, practice questions, websites, etc.)

From all that information, what should be included in your notes? If information is included in two of these sources, make sure it is in your notes. If it is in three or more of these sources, be sure it's in your notes in a *memorable way*. You can be fairly certain you will be asked to recall it again on a test.

Let's Talk about Highlighting

Some students consider highlighting a form of note-making. Sorry. It isn't. It does not organize the information and is too passive. When you highlight one word or phrase, it says, "Look at me!" But when you highlight most of a page, you have too much information competing for your attention. "Look at me!" "No! Look at me!" "Hey! What about me?" "Over here!" "Don't forget about me!"

Too much highlighting makes it hard to see what is truly important.

The key is to use highlighting sparingly, so you can hear it "calling to you." The best highlighters are very selective in what they mark. Vocabulary words are good to highlight. Important ideas that you see repeatedly can be highlighted. You may also want to highlight a detail or concept in your charts.

You may wonder, "Okay, highlighting may not be enough, but why can't I make notes like I always have? Why do I need a set of what you call highly-organized and condensed notes?"

Glad you asked!

Why You Should Make Great Notes

> A busy schedule doesn't allow for repeated reading of the text—even if it's only what you highlighted. Highly organized notes set you free from your textbooks and can be reviewed quickly and repeatedly. (Remember, repetition is the key to memory.)

> The act of creating your own set of structured notes makes the information your own. What makes it your own is your analysis of what is important, how the details relate to the main topics and using your own words.

> You can't self-test from high-lighted passages, notes made in the margins or from your hand-outs. You need to be able to self-test because self-testing lets you know if you're prepared for an exam—or not.

> While great notes may take longer to create, learning the information for the long term saves time by

not having to keep re-learning information and allows you to build in guilt-free rewards to enjoy.

> Creating a great set of notes is a more effective *and* more efficient way to use your time.

Rules for Making Study Notes

> Include all **essential** information on the topic.

> **Organize** your notes into a format that shows relationships between topics, subtopics and details. Name and location? Cause and effect? Compare and contrast? Time sequence or process? Broad concepts?

> Make it **visually interesting** by using colors and white space.

> **Condense** material for repeated review.

> Use **your own** words.

> Choose a format that allows **self-testing.**

⟩⟩ Four Major Note Types

Flash Cards

You probably are already making flash cards. But are you using them in the best way? Cards are helpful for repeated reviews of simple details. For example, vocabulary words and their definitions, short lists and formulas make good use of flash cards. Other note types are better suited for longer or more complex information.

In case you're not already making flash cards in the best way, here's a quick review for making them by hand:

> Use both sides of the cards. One side will be for the question, the other for the answer.

> Keep it simple. Too much information makes cards hard to review.

Example of a Flash Card

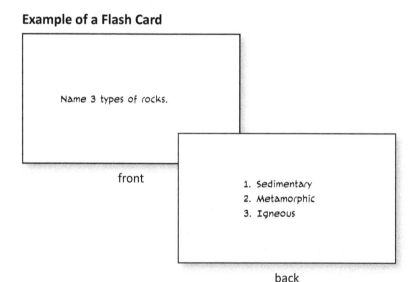

Name 3 types of rocks.

front

1. Sedimentary
2. Metamorphic
3. Igneous

back

It's easy to self-test with cards and you can carry them with you anywhere—either on paper or electronically.

How to Use Your Flash Cards   You can group paper cards by subject, using a rubber band or putting them on a ring to hold them together. Some students choose to use different colored cards for each topic or class. For example your Geology cards could be green, your Psychology cards could be blue, etc. See if your electronic flash cards also allow color coding.

To self-test from flash cards, you simply read the question on one side, then say, think or write the answer and turn the card over to check if you were right.

If you answered correctly, put the card in your "know" pile. If not, then it goes into the "don't know" pile. Keep sorting through the "don't know" pile until all cards are all transferred to the "know" pile. This method will keep you from spending time on information you have already mastered. Electronic versions typically have a way to determine how often you review the cards. If you knew the information on the card, you can review it later, but if you didn't know the information, then you need to review it again quickly, in a few minutes, if possible.

Always carry cards from your "don't know" stack (10–20 cards is typical). You can do many quick reviews during the day by using the time between classes or while waiting for something or someone. Most students find that they can usually work in at least five reviews during the day. That night you should be able to sort them one last time and happily put the cards in your "know" pile!

At this rate, you will have mastered 50–100 new details by the end of the week. During a 15-week semester that could add up to 700–1500 factoids!

Keep in mind that several short review sessions are much better for long-term retention than one long "slog."

Advantages of Cards	Disadvantages of Cards
Easy to capture isolated bits of information you must master.	Lose the context, as it is not embedded in a larger picture.
Easy to make.	Can get "carried away" and try to make all your notes on cards.
Easy to sort and use for self testing.	
Easy to carry in your pocket or on your phone.	

Category Charts

Category charts are useful in so many courses that they are frequently used in textbooks to summarize information. Sometimes teachers also prepare charts as handouts.

When the task is to *compare and contrast* information, category charts are the way to go.

If you needed to know more detail about the three types of rocks, used as an example in the section on flash cards, you could make a category chart like the one below.

Example of a Category Chart

Types of rocks	Formation	Common subtypes
Sedimentary	Formed by wind and water	Clastic Sand and sandstone Rock asphalt Ironstone Evaporites −carbonates −siliceous rocks
Igneous	Created by volcanoes and undersea fissures	Feldspar Quartz Pyroxine Olivene Mica
Metamorphic	Created when igneous or sedimentary rocks are transformed by pressure or heat into denser, more compacted rock	Slate Schist Gneiss Marble

In a typical chart, the names you need to remember are placed in the far left column and the details are placed in boxes across the top row.

As you can see, there is a difference between the amount of information on a flash card and on a category chart. How can you decide whether the information deserves just a flash card or if a category chart is a better choice? One way to determine if the added details are important is whether they appear in two or more of the resources: book, lecture, course objectives or handouts.

Hint: If your instructors took the time to include the information in your course syllabus, objectives, or handout, you should probably make a chart.

Examples of Students' Charts   Following are some student-made charts which show how others have organized the informa-

Advantages of Category Charts	Disadvantages of Category Charts
Research shows that using this format helps you remember more information than other note types.	Category charts take longer to make than loose notes because you have to think about the organization. But, really, that's a good thing!
Category charts show the relationship between main ideas and details.	
Category charts provide a context in which to remember the details. Context improves understanding and recall.	
Review is simple, especially compared to re-reading the text.	
Using this format, it is possible to quickly test yourself over a lot of information	
The visual impact of a chart makes it memorable.	
The analysis and evaluation required to make charts promotes critical thinking skills.	
Category charts are the only note type that gives feedback. If one of the boxes in the chart is empty, you know that information is missing.	

tion they needed to learn. These study aids may give you ideas on how you might want to make your own notes. Warning: there may be factual errors in these sample charts, so do not plan to use them for your own studies without first checking them for accuracy. Also note that students sometimes use their own short-hand to save space, e.g., ↓ for decrease, ↑ for increase, ~ for about, etc.

Look at how these charts are organized. Do you see why the student chose the particular structure? Your own charts may be organized differently from these examples. That's fine. Charts are personalized and individualized learning tools. They should make sense to YOU and help YOU remember what's important to know.

Chart 3.1   The XII Cranial Nerves

	Name	Origin & Course	Function	Clinical Testing	Illustrate	Other
I	Olfactory (Smell)	Arise from olfactory receptor cells in olfactory epithelium cribriform plate of ethnoid bone synapse in olfactory bulb	Sensory (afferent impulses)	Sniff different scents		Anosmia = loss of smell
II	Optic (Vision)	Arise from retina to form optic nerve → thru optic canal of orbit.	Sensory (afferent impulses)	Vision & visual fields. Fundus viewed w/ ophthalmoscope		Anopsias = visual defects or partial loss of vision
III	Oculomotor (Eye 'mover')	Extend from ventral midbrain → bony orbit via superior orbital fissure	Chiefly Motor; a few proprioceptive afferents: –Somatic –Parasympathetic –Sensory	Pupils size, shape, equality & reflex. Convergence & ability to follow objects w/ eyes.		At rest, eye rotates laterally; upper eyelid droops; double vision; trouble focusing up close.
IV	Trochlear (Eye 'pulley')	Emerge from dorsal midbrain → ventrally around midbrain → orbit thru superior orbital fissure w/ oculomotor nerves	Primarily Motor; somatic motor fibers to / proprioceptor fibers from the superior oblique muscle	Tested in common with III. See above.		Injury = double vision and reduced ability to move eye.

* Illustrations from Gray's Anatomy via Wikimedia. http://commons.wikimedia.org/wiki/Gray%27s_Anatomy_plates

Chart 3.2   The XII Cranial Nerves, continued

	Name	Origin & Course	Function	Clinical Testing	Illustrate	Other
V	Trigeminal					
V₁	Ophthalmic					
V₂	Maxillary					
V₃	Mandibular					
VI	Abducens (turns eye laterally)					
VII	Facial					
VIII	Vestibulocochlear (hearing & balance)					
IX	Glossophar-yngeal (tongue & pharynx)					
X	Vagus (thorax & abdomen)					Only CN to go beyond head & neck
XI	Accessory	Union of cranial root & spinal root				
XII	Hypoglossal (under tongue)					

Note: As shown in this chart, make sure to label the chart and the columns when a chart is longer than one page.

Chart 3.3 Electrical & Chemical Synapses

	Definition	Structure / Gap Junction	Function / Speed / Plasticity	Direction / Gain / Size
Chemical Synapse	Predominant kind Functional connections between neurons &/or other types of cells (muscles / glands) Site of action for majority of psychoactive drugs	Asymmetric in structure Gap junction / nexus junction= cells approach w/in 20–40 nm (called a synaptic cleft)	Post-synaptic potential caused by opening of ion channels by chem. transmitters Produce complex behaviors Slower than elec. delay = 2ms	Direction (?) Have gain Relative neuron size has no importance
Electrical Synapse	Mechan & elec. conductive link b'tween 2 neuron cells — gap junction	Gap junction= cells approach w/in 3.5nm (much closer than chem.)	Direct electrical coupling b'tween neurons Often found in neural systems / retina /cerebral cortex Produce simple, but quick behaviors Faster than chem. delay = 0.2 ms Evidence of plasticity	Typically bi-directional Do not have gain Small pre-synaptic cell cannot produce much effect in larger post-synaptic cell

Chart 3.4 Personality Disorders

Personality Disorder	Description	DSM Criteria	Class of Disorder
Paranoid	General distrust and suspiciousness of others.	• Suspect others are harming them (without evidence) • Doubt the loyalty or trustworthiness of others • Afraid to confide in others b/c info may be used against them • Sense threatening or insulting meanings in benign remarks/events • Unforgiving/Hold grudges • Perceive attacks on one's character and quick to anger	Odd/eccentric ; highly comorbid and 2.1% have been diagnosed
Histrionic	Excessive need for attention, superficial and fleeting emotions, and impulsivity	• Discomfort in situations where they are not the center of attention • Emotions shift rapidly and do not seem "real" • Speech characterized by unsupported "impressions" • Suggestible and easily influenced • Inappropriately provocative or sexually seductive towards others • Very dramatic behavior and expression of emotions • Consider relationships much more intimate and close than they are	Dramatic; present in 5.5% of population, highly comorbid
Narcissistic	Marked by grandiosity, arrogance, and a tendency to exploit others	• Extreme sense of self-importance • Belief that one's uniqueness is only understood by high-status people • Excessive need for admiration • Extreme sense of entitlement • Lack of empathy for others • Frequent envy or belief that others envy them • Arrogant behavior and attitude	Dramatic; present in 5.5% of population, highly comorbid
Obsessive-compulsive	Rigidity, perfectionism and strong need for control.	• Preoccupation w/ details, organization, and rules • Hoarder • Perfectionism interferes with task completion • Over-conscientiousness and inflexibility regarding morality and ethics • Reluctance to let go and delegate tasks	Anxiety/ Fearful occur in 2.3% of pop.

Chart 3.5   RNA Types

Type of RNA	Abbreviation	Purpose / Found
Ribosomal	rRNA	Found in ribosomes. ~ 85% of cellular RNA
Transfer	tRNA	Adaptor molecules link aa's to genetic code. ~ 10% of cellular RNA
Messenger	mRNA	Carries messages from DNA → ribosome for translation
Small (Eukaryotes)	snRNA	Aids in splicing of hnRNA in nucleus. In cytosol, miRNAs regulate translation of mRNA targets
Micro	miRNA	Regulators that bind to mRNA. Do bad things to mRNA. Translation repression. premiRNA → Dicer → miRNA

Chart 3.6 Microbiology Case Study

Pathogen	S/S	Pt. History	Treatment	Prognosis	Vaccine?	Other
Methicillin-resistant staphylococcus aureus (MRSA)	Physical Exam: • Leg pain / swelling • Necrotic lesions • ROM normal	19 yr old male Athlete	Proper skin care	Varies based on severity.	No	Furuncle (boils) caused by staph aureus in hair follicles.
		Chills / pain while walking	Surgical procedure to open sores	Good, if not MRSA.		
	Vital Signs: • Elevated temp • BP normal • Elevated pulse • Elevated respir.	Tender, painful boils		Difficulty in determining effective antibiotic, can complicate treatment.		Surge of WBC sent to fight bacterium. Infection not fought off quickly enough.
		Took Amoxicillin, but no effect.	Antibiotics			
	Lab Results: • Normal hematocrit • Elevated WBC & eosinophils • Elevated CD4					MRSA resistant to Amoxicillin.

Tips on Making Your Own Category Charts

> If you didn't draft a chart while pre-reading, you can begin making a tentative chart during lecture.

> Wait until after you have gathered all the necessary information (been to lecture and read the text) on that topic before making the *final* version of your chart.

> How the syllabus, lecture and text are organized will give you ideas on how to organize your chart. For example, if the syllabus says "compare and contrast aerobic and anaerobic bacteria," a category chart would work well.

> Use the charts in the text or handouts in addition to making your own. They can be used for review and self-tests.

> The maximum number for categories (columns or rows) is five to seven. More than that becomes too much to review quickly.

> The first column (far left) on each chart should contain the name of the subject/topic/main category. The other columns will provide the types of details. Actual details are in the boxes.

> You should be able to review each chart in five minutes or less. Repetition = Retention.

> When a lecturer makes a point of saying something that is not in your book, or if he or she disagrees with a portion of the text or adds in new information, put that in your notes!

> Some topics have information that doesn't fit your chosen categories. When this happens it's a good idea to have "other" or "miscellaneous" as the last column to capture any important information that doesn't fit elsewhere on your chart.

> The information in the boxes of your chart should be concise. It is there to remind you of the complete information you have already studied and know.

> Make your charts visually attractive. If they look good, you'll be

more likely to enjoy reviewing them, and you'll be more likely to remember the content. Use color. Be neat. Use white space.

> The textbook will usually organize information in a logical progression. You can often lay out the main categories in your chart according to that same format.

> Sticky notes can be used to plan charts. If there are very many, you can stick them on a wall or mirror and move them around until they are in a logical order.

> You can also use a whiteboard (dry erase board) to sketch out the categories as you plan your chart.

> Be forewarned! Creating a chart is often a messy process, involving trial-and-error, as you choose what information will be included. That's okay. It is the very process of choosing how to organize the information that begins to build a mental model and which makes the chart (and the information) memorable. Making charts quickly and accurately gets easier with practice. You are forming the habit of looking at information in a logical way from the beginning as you pre-read.

> In the interest of saving time, students in study groups sometimes divide the job of creating charts among themselves. They then distribute copies of their charts to the other group members. If you choose to do this, double check for accuracy and plan to spend more time in review. Most students tell us they would rather make their own charts. The effort expended to organize the information makes it theirs. Students tell us it's the act of making the charts that increases comprehension and embeds the information in their memory.

> A variation on the idea above is to have the small group create the chart together. This can help the group work in a more organized and efficient way. If you use a dry erase board to create the group chart, then each person can take a picture of

the completed chart and use it for continued review and self-test.

> You WILL remember what is on your chart, so be sure that the information is accurate. It's hard to erase facts from your memory once they've been learned and repeated.

> Charts can be made either by hand or on the computer. If you develop a template you can print or copy it and use it repeatedly. (You can often begin to fill in a chart template during pre-reading, reading or lecture.)

Not Just for Facts: Learning Concepts with Category Charts   Sometimes a student will ask if a category chart (or matrix) can be used for learning concepts as well as facts. The answer is, "Yes!"

Research done by Susan Markle and Phillip Tiemann describes how concept-learning takes place.

Understanding a Concept   A student understands a concept when:

1. Given term, he gives definition
2. Given definition, he gives term
3. Given an example, she names the concept
4. Given a concept, she gives examples
5. Given non-example, he identifies it as a non-example
6. Given two concepts, she compares and contrasts them by saying what each is (definition) and noting the difference
7. Given examples from multiple concepts, he can classify all of them

We have taken Markle and Tiemann's criteria and created a category chart. See Chart 3.7.

Chart 3.7 Learning Concepts Category Chart

Name of Concept / Classification	Definition	Examples (Generalize)	Non-Example (Discriminate)	Other

Why Not Just Make Outlines? Why don't we recommend outlining as one of our note-making methods?

> Outlines tend to become loose notes, that is, disorganized. Though students may think they are outlining according to a hierarchical structure, they often abandon the formal outline and just end up with pages of unstructured information.

> Anything that can be outlined can be charted. Charts, however, are vastly superior to outlines for learning, reviewing and self-testing, as you will see in Step 4. The act of creating a chart helps you recall more of the information and charts make reviewing and self-testing so easy, you will be glad you took the time to make them.

The next two pages show an example of turning an outline into a chart.

Outline of Three Major Nutrients—Proteins, Fats and Carbohydrates

I. Proteins
   A. Purpose
      1. Growth
      2. Tissue repair
      3. Immune function
      4. Making essential hormones and enzymes

5. Energy when carbs not available
6. Preserving lean muscle mass
B. Function
Proteins are broken into amino acids. Some amino acids are essential—must come from our diet. Protein from animal sources contains all the essential amino acids needed.
C. Sources
1. Meats (including poultry and fish)
2. Cheese and other dairy products
3. Legumes (beans)

II. Fats / (Lipids)
A. Purpose
1. Normal growth and development
2. Energy
3. Absorption of Vitamins A, D, E, K and carotenoids
4. Maintains cell membranes
5. Brain functioning
6. Satiety
B. Function
Fats needed for the proper absorption of some vitamins and for normal growth and development. Fats from natural sources are more healthful than trans fats. Trans fats are commonly found in baked goods, snack foods and fried foods.
C. Sources
1. Meats
2. Nuts
3. Dairy products
4. Olive oil
5. Commercially prepared baked goods and snack foods.

III. Carbohydrates
A. Purpose
1. Main source of fuel / energy
2. Stored in muscles and liver
3. Fibrous foods promote good intestinal health
B. Function
Carbohydrates are main source of energy. Fast or simple carbs can cause blood sugar levels to spike then drop, so simple carbs need added protein or fat. Slow or complex carbs do not cause blood sugar levels to fluctuate—preferred source of carbs.
C. Sources
1. Simple carbs: sugars, honey, fruit juices, puffed cereals, foods made with white flour
2. Complex carbs: green leafy and/or colorful vegetables, whole grains, some fruits.

Chart of Three Major Nutrients—Proteins, Fats and Carbohydrates

	Purpose	Function	Sources	Other
Proteins	1. Growth 2. Tissue repair 3. Immune function 4. Make essential hormones and enzymes 5. Energy when carbs not available 6. Preserve lean muscle mass	Our bodies break down the protein into amino acids. Some amino acids are essential, which means that we need to get them from our diet. Protein that comes from animal sources contains all the essential amino acids that we need.	• Meats (including poultry and fish) • Cheese and other dairy products • Legumes (beans)	
Fats/Lipids	1. Normal growth and development 2. Energy 3. Absorption of Vitamins A, D, E, K and carotenoids 4. Maintains cell membranes 5. Brain functioning 6. Satiety	Fats are needed for the proper absorption of vitamins ADEK and for normal growth / development. Fats from natural sources are more healthful than trans fats. Trans fats are commonly found in baked goods, snack foods and fried foods.	• Meats • Nuts • Dairy products • Olive oil • Commercially prepared baked goods and snack foods (trans fats)	
Carbohydrates	1. Main source of fuel / energy 2. Stored in muscles and liver 3. Fibrous foods promote good intestinal health	Carbohydrates are typically our bodies' main source of energy. Fast or simple carbs can cause blood sugar levels to spike then drop, so you should also eat some protein or fat with simple carbs. Slow or complex carbs do not cause blood sugar levels to fluctuate, so this is the preferred source of carbs.	• Simple carbs: sugars, honey, fruit juices, puffed cereals, white flour • Complex carbs: green leafy and/or colorful vegetables, whole grain products and whole fruits.	

It's interesting to compare how the information is organized in these two note types (outline vs. category chart). The information in the chart is the same, but it takes up less space and even has room for more information to be added later. Research by Kiewra and others has shown that category charts make information more memorable.

Advantages of Charts over Outlines   There really are no disadvantages.

> Category charts are the only note type that let you know if information is missing. If a box is empty, it's a signal that you need to locate that information.

> The structure of a category chart organizes information in a highly memorable way.

> The similarities and differences among the details are the types of information that tend to appear on exams.

> Multiple choice questions are so easy to make from a chart that you might as well study the same information that way.

> A well-made chart is laid out so that the differences among the details inside the boxes are unmistakable.

> It's difficult to self-test from an outline but easy from a chart.

How to Know When a Category Chart Is the Best Type of Note
When the information involves more than one category of subtopic and more than one detail connected to each subtopic, a category chart is recommended.

Below are some cue words that signal a category chart is probably your best choice:

> category

> compare

> contrast

> types of

> differences between / among

> similarities between / among

> factors, (discuss factors affecting . . .)

Flowcharts

A flowchart shows the sequence, development or results of a process over time. If movement or change is involved, a flowchart is a good choice for your study note. Examples include: physiological processes like blood clotting or wound healing or steps in formation of rock types, clouds or chemical processes.

How do you create a flowchart? The first event or stage in the process is placed at the top or left of the page with an arrow leading to the second event or stage. In a flowchart the details are at the end of each arrow, and you may also box them or use color for greater visual impact.

Most students draw flowcharts by hand, as it helps embed the information in their memory, but you may want to consider using software that will help you create flowcharts.

Advantages of Flowcharts	Disadvantages of Flowcharts
You can see the details in relation to each other and to the main topic.	Only useful for information that occurs in a temporal sequence or changes over time.
The clear visual picture is memorable and easy to review.	
Easy to use for self-testing.	
It's the only way to make a condensed note for some types of information.	

How to Decide When to Use a Flowchart   Flowcharts involve a sequence of events, processes or changes over time. Below are some cue words that signal a flowchart might be your best choice:

> circulation

> cycle

> flow

> movement

> phase

> process

> sequence

> cascade

> progression

> timeline

Flowchart 3.1   Binary Fission

DNA replication

Chromosome segregation

Cytokinesis

Flowchart 3.2   Biogenesis of miRNAs

1. Transcription by Pol II

↓

2. Hairpin release in the nucleus

↓

3. Export to cytoplasm

↓

4. Dicer processing

↓

5. Strand selection

↓

6. Formation of RISC (RNA-induced silencing complex).
Translation repression.

Diagrams

Diagrams are drawings or illustrations that show features of an object. They are probably the most common illustrations you will find in your textbooks.

A diagram is used when you are expected to know the name, location or structure of an object.

You can either copy diagrams from the text or related websites or draw them free hand. Here's where your artistic side can really shine! How you label the parts is the key to its usefulness for review and self-test.

Labeling to make self-testing easier:

1. The parts of the diagrams should be numbered or lettered.
2. Draw a line from the numbered part out to the side (a couple of inches, at least) where you will write the name of the numbered part.
3. Cover the names on the side when you self-test.

Diagrams may not be the easiest type of note for self-testing. Covering the labels with scrap paper, (or making additional copies without the answers) and writing what should be on the underlying label, makes review and self-testing easier. Many students tell us that, as with the other structured note forms, it is the act of grappling with the information while creating the diagram that makes the information memorable.

So we could show you more detailed examples, these diagrams were retrieved from Wikipedia.

Diagram 3.1   Cell Membrane

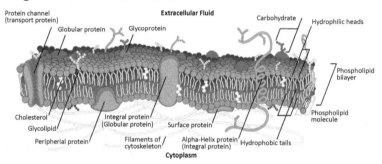

http://commons.wikimedia.org/wiki/File:Cell_membrane_detailed_diagram_en.svg#mediaviewer/File:Cell_membrane_detailed_diagram_en.svg

Diagram 3.2   Plant Cell Structure

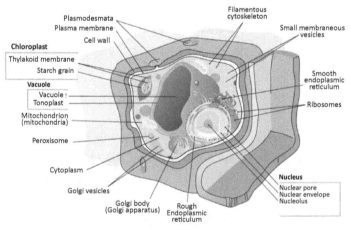

http://commons.wikimedia.org/wiki/File:Plant_cell_structure_svg.svg#mediaviewer/File:Plant_cell_structure_svg.svg

Combined Note Forms

Combined note forms use elements of two or more of the previously-discussed kinds of notes.

For many topics you may find that combining note forms make sense. Students sometimes include a drawing on their flash cards to help jog their memory. Other examples are inserting a flowchart or diagram in a category chart, as illustrated in the XII Cranial Nerves chart, or using a flash card for a very simple flowchart or category chart.

Combination Diagram & Flowchart 3.1 Flu Virus

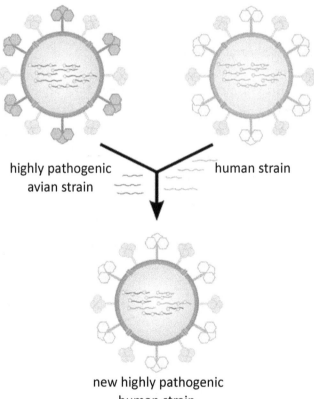

highly pathogenic
avian strain

human strain

new highly pathogenic
human strain

How to Choose Which Note Type

The decision table "How to Choose a Note Type" located in the summary of the chapter will help you decide how to choose the best type of note for your purpose. The table summarizes the different types of notes discussed in this chapter and nicely illustrates the usefulness of category charts. ☺

In the meantime, the next three examples will give you some ideas about how to decide whether to make a flowchart, diagram or category chart.

Let's say your American History class is studying the Revolutionary War. One of the battles fought was the Battle of Fort Washington in November 1776. If your teacher (or syllabus) says you need to know the placement of the troops during that engagement, then you might choose a combination diagram and flow chart as illustrated below.

Battle of Fort Washington 1776 (Combined Diagram & Flowchart)

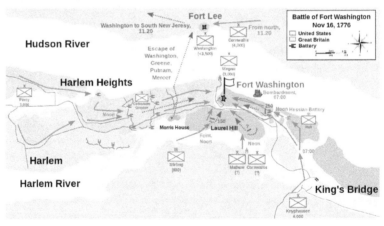

http://commons.wikimedia.org/wiki/File:Battle_of_Fort_Washington,_1776.svg#mediaviewer/File:Battle_of_Fort_Washington,_1776.svg

Or perhaps your instructor wants you to know the layout of Fort Washington. In that case a diagram, like the one below would be a good choice.

Layout of Fort Washington (Diagram)

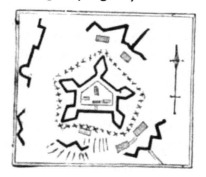

http://commons.wikimedia.org/wiki/File:Fort_
Washington_Lossing.png#mediaviewer/File:Fort_
Washington_Lossing.png

If your professor asked you to learn about the major participants, their leaders, how many soldiers were involved and the outcome, then you would likely choose to create a category chart like the one below.

Battle of Fort Washington (Category Chart)

Date	November 16, 1776
Location	Washington Heights, Manhattan, New York
Result	British victory

Belligerents	Commanders & Leaders	Strength	Wounded / Killed	Captured
United States	George Washington Robert Magaw Nathanael Greene	3,000	59 / 96	2,837
vs.				
Great Britain	William Howe Hugh Percy	8,000	84 / 37	Unknown
Hesse-Kassel	Wilhelm von Knyphausen			

Do you see from these examples how the type of information to be learned will determine the type of note that you make? (E.g., movement = flow chart; static location = diagram; multiple categories to compare = category chart.)

Mapping

Mapping is a pictorial tool used to arrange complex topics. Maps look a little like flowcharts but they are multi-directional. This is not one of the note types that we recommend because while it shows relationships, it does not promote storage of information in long-term memory.

Maps are known by a variety of names: concept maps, networks, knowledge maps or process maps. They are typically used to deal with connections or relationships among concepts or themes and are most often used at the highest level of generality. For example, they may be used as an introduction to a new topic or in summary of a recently discussed topic.

Both students and teachers have used them to summarize an entire course. But on objective exams you are not typically asked big picture or general questions. Exam questions typically focus

Advantages of Maps	Disadvantages of Maps
Useful to capture knowledge or summarize what is already known about a subject that is complex and covers a wide scope (e.g., an entire course or textbook).	To include the necessary details, additional maps need to be created, which interferes with the goal of condensing the amount of information you have to learn.
Helpful in illustrating relationships across topics or disciplines.	Maps do not provide the level of detail that typically appears on examinations.
Maps can be used to introduce a topic or give an overview or summary of the course.	Lack the inherent structure to make the information memorable.
	The proponents of mapping, as well as the structure itself, discourage memorization.

Concept Map 3.1   Concept Mapping

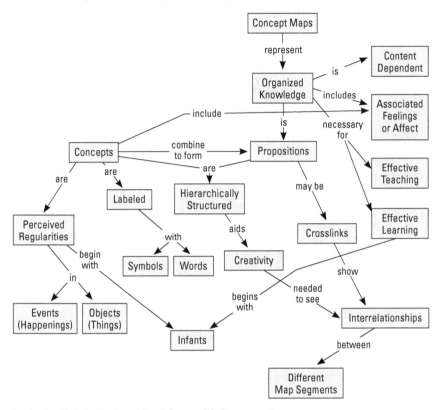

Based on: http://upload.wikimedia.org/wikipedia/commons/3/3a/Conceptmap.gif

on details, which are not easily learned by mapping. If you are asked to write an essay on a topic, however, a map could be useful.

How Can I Make Notes if I Don't Understand the Topic?

It's true that you must have some understanding before you can begin making your notes. The following lists will walk you through the steps to improve your comprehension of any topic.

What to Do When You Don't Understand—Old School Book-Based Method

1. Go to the library.
2. Find the shelf with textbooks on the subject you don't understand.
3. Choose three to five text books which cover the topic.
4. Select recent editions, those with colorful illustrations, or one with an attractive, appealing layout.
5. Sit down at a large table and open all the books to the specific topic you want to understand better.
6. Read the explanation given in each of the books.
7. Stop when it becomes clear and summarize what you learned in some form of note.

What to Do When You Don't Understand— Computer-Based Method

1. Go a computer lab. (Unless you have 2-3 monitors of your own.)
2. Sit down at a place with two (or three) computer monitors.
3. Search on the subject/topic you don't understand. (Start with Wikipedia and/or YouTube.)
4. Choose three to five promising-looking resources.
5. Select those with colorful illustrations or animations, or one

with an appealing visual component. Choose at least one resource with sound, (i.e., someone talking you through it, if appropriate), and at least one that animates or demonstrates the process you are trying to understand.

6. One at a time, watch / read / listen to the explanation given on each of the sites.
7. Stop when it becomes clear and summarize what you learned in some form of note.

Note: Having multiple monitors allows you to quickly scan several resources at once. Using only one monitor and opening and closing screens or tabs removes the visual impact and lessens the benefit of this exercise.

Why Does This Work?

Every resource explains the topic somewhat differently. Each author will take a slightly different approach, and one of these should click with you. The "aha!" may be an illustration, or an animation, so make sure you look at those, too.

Some people hypothesize that looking at several resources works because of the repetitive nature and cumulative effect. Whatever the reason, it works! So give it a try next time you are feeling stuck.

Scheduling Time to Make Good Notes

Your notes are central to the Six Steps study system. You can't review and self-test easily without a good set of notes. It's important to take the time—whatever time it takes—to make a good set of notes. The act of creating the notes embeds the information in your brain. These notes will be used repeatedly to review for quizzes, exams, finals, and maybe even standardized exams. They are worth the investment. Students find these note making strategies more engaging and often say things like, "I never knew that making notes could be fun!" and "I was really proud of the notes I made. I enjoyed reviewing from them."

Storing Digital Files

These days, few faculty allow the excuse of, "My computer crashed!" as a reason for turning in late work. They expect you to have saved your assignments in multiple locations. You will want to create a backup of your course notes, too.

Some possible backup resources, in addition to your computer's hard drive, include:

> External hard drive
> USB drive
> Dropbox
> Evernote
> Google Drive
> Microsoft OneDrive
> Your favorite? _____

For storing your digital notes, set up a course folder and have sub-folders organized by chapter and topic. For example: Chem 101, Dr. Frank N. Stein / Chapter & Topic

Chapter 1: Chemistry and the Atomic/Molecular View of Matter
Chapter 2: Scientific Measurements

Chapter 3: Elements, Compounds, and the Periodic Table

Chapter 4: The Mole and Stoichiometry

The notes you create will go in the appropriate chapter/topic folder.

Storing Paper Notes

Here are some ideas:

Type of Note	Paper Storage
Note Cards	File boxes with tabs for each course and each major topic within the course.
	Small file boxes, like recipe boxes, for each course.
	Banded with rubber bands or on ring for each course or topic within a course.
Category Charts	File folders by course.
	Three-ring binders with tabs for each course and each major topic within the course or material between exams for a course.
Flow Charts	File folders by course.
	Three-ring binders with tabs for each course and each major topic within the course.
Diagrams	File folders by course.
	Three-ring binders with tabs for each course and each major topic within the course.
Combined Note Forms	File folders by course.
	Three-ring binders with tabs for each course and each major topic within the course.
Maps	File folders by course.
	Three-ring binders with tabs for each course and each major topic within the course.

Act
Reading and Note-Making

For the next week, schedule one to two study periods each week-day and another study period on the weekend. Especially at the beginning of a semester, note-making will be your main study activity outside of lecture. Make as many different types of notes as the material permits, including flash cards, category charts, flowcharts, diagrams and combined charts.

The amount of time needed to study for each course will depend on the difficulty of the information and what you already know about the topic, but one to two hours of personal study per classroom hour continues to be a reasonable guideline. **Remember: the goal of note-making is to free yourself from the book and other assigned materials and have only one source for review and self-test.** Your final set of study notes should include everything you absolutely need to know. Students tell us that they get much faster with practice and learn to make mental notes and connections as new information is encountered. In the research literature, this is known as "reach and reciprocity"—the act of incorporating new information (reach) into your current base of knowledge (reciprocity).

You will start to think in a different way and will:

> notice the type of information and how it is organized
> be more alert to what information is important
> observe which details support the main idea
> see patterns, similarities and differences
> analyze and evaluate the information you are reading
> discover new insights or new applications.

Some educators call this process critical thinking. You might also think of it as careful thinking. In the learning process we teach, critical thinking begins with pre-reading.

Study Environment

If you find you are having difficulty studying because of noise or visual distractions, skip ahead to the chapter about concentration (Step 5) and implement some of the strategies that will help you create a good study environment. Improved concentration increases what you remember and can often decrease the length of your study periods!

After one week of practicing these note-making strategies, complete the Check-up Exercise below. You may continue with the next step (Review and Self-test) during that time.

Act & Analyze

Check-up

Reading and Note-Making Exercise

1. List the different types of notes you made for each class.

_____

_____

_____

2. Did you understand the material better after you made the notes? If so, why?

_____

_____

_____

3. What difficulties, if any, did you encounter?

_____

_____

_____

4. How did this process begin to change the way you think about the information?

_____

_____

_____

Adjust

Write the name of the class in which you plan to make a variety of note types this semester. Experiment with the type of note that best condenses and organizes the information you are learning. Use the category chart (matrix) format as your default. Kiewra and others have found that notes organized as category charts (matrices) help students remember more information than other types of notes.

_____

⟩⟩ Summary

Preparing for Lecture: Good / Better / Best

	Activity before Lecture	Time
Good	• Pre-read • Make Flash Cards	5 to 15 minutes
Better	• Pre-read • Make Flash Cards • Read the Assignment	30 to 60 minutes
Best	• Pre-read • Make Flash Cards • Read the Assignment • Make Structured Notes or Work Problems	1 to 2 hours

Note-making is the heart and soul of the Six Steps study system.

Good Notes

> Increase comprehension. You can't make a good set of notes without understanding the material.

> Save time. You have only one thing (your notes) to review.

> Build-in self testing. No need to create additional materials for quizzing yourself.

> Focus your attention. Helps you condense what you need to know by combining information from multiple sources.

> Help you become a critical thinker. You can distinguish what is important in the midst of much detailed information and see relationships among the details.

Note Making vs. Note Taking

Did you notice that we use the term note-making and not note-taking? There is a difference. We want you to get in the habit of creating your own notes and not relying on information that others have put together. *Science Daily* reports that Mickes and Harris have found that notes in your own words are more memorable, too.

Decision Table 3.1   How To Choose a Note Type

Note Type	Type of Information
Flash Card	Simple details, facts, vocabulary words (and definitions), or short lists
Category Chart	Compared and contrasted
	More than one category of sub-topic and more than one type of detail for each sub-topic
Flowchart	Multiple steps or decisions
	A process
Diagram	Names, locations, or arrangement of parts of an object or structure
A combination of the above formats to match the information types	Combination of the above information types
Map **Note:** *Maps often become other types of notes.*	Deals with connections or relationships among concepts or themes at a high level of generality

)) References

Battle of Fort Washington, 1776. By Oneam - Own work. Licensed under Creative Commons Attribution-Share Alike 3.0 via Wikimedia Commons.
http://commons.wikimedia.org/wiki/File:Battle_of_Fort_Washington,_1776.svg#mediaviewer/File:Battle_of_Fort_Washington,_1776.svg

Bruner, J.S. (1961). The act of discovery. *Harvard Educational Review*, 31, 21–32.

The importance of organizers in remembering and recalling information. The act of making your own notes or organizers is a big part of the learning process.

Cell membrane detailed diagram. By LadyofHats Mariana Ruiz - Own work. Image renamed from File:Cell membrane detailed diagram. svg. Licensed under Public domain via Wikimedia Commons.
http://commons.wikimedia.org/wiki/File:Cell_membrane_detailed_diagram_en.svg#mediaviewer/File:Cell_membrane_detailed_diagram_en.svg

Clark, R. C. & Lyons, C. (2004). *Graphics for learning*. San Francisco: Pfeiffer, 133–138.

Studies show that using charts (matrices) to study information increases retention by 10–20% over reading the text or studying an outline.

Concept Map. By Vicwood40 [GFDL (http://www.gnu.org/copyleft/fdl .html) or CC-BY-SA-3.0 (http://creativecommons.org/licenses/ by-sa/3.0/)], via Wikimedia Commons.
http://upload.wikimedia.org/wikipedia/commons/3/3a /Conceptmap.gif

Foshay, W.R., Silber, K.H. & Stelnicki, M.B. (2003) *Writing training materials that work*. San Francisco: Jossey-Bass/Pfeiffer.

A guide based on current cognitive psychology and instructional design theory and research. This book addresses creating instructional materials, which is what students do when they create study notes for their own learning.

Fort Washington Lossing. By Benson John Lossing. Licensed under Public domain via Wikimedia Commons. http://commons.wikimedia.org/wiki/File:Fort_Washington_ Lossing.png#mediaviewer/File:Fort_Washington_Lossing.png

Influenza Genetic Shift. By Influenza_geneticshift.jpg: Dhorspool at en.wikipediaderivative work: Jiver - This file was derived from:Influenza_geneticshift.jpg. Licensed under Creative Commons Attribution-Share Alike 3.0 via Wikimedia Commons. http://commons.wikimedia.org/wiki/File:Influenza_geneticshift .svg#mediaviewer/File:Influenza_geneticshift.svg

Jairam, D., & Kiewra, K. (2010). Helping students SOAR to success on computers: An investigation of the SOAR study method for computer-based learning. *Journal of Educational Psychology*, Vol. 102, No. 3, 601–614.

Katayama, A.D., Robinson, D.H. (2000). Getting students "partially" involved in note-taking using graphic organizers. *The Journal of Experimental Education*, Volume 68, Issue 2, 2000, pages 119–133. DOI: 10.1080/00220970009598498

College students studied a chapter-length text along with a set of complete, partial, or skeletal graphic organizers or outlines. Two days later, the students reviewed their materials for 10 min and then completed factual and application tests. On the factual test, there was no effect for either study notes or amount of information. However, on the application test, graphic organizers were better than outlines and partial notes were better than complete notes.

Kauffman, D.F., & Kiewra, K.A. (2010). What makes a matrix so effective? An empirical test of the relative benefits of signaling, extraction, and localization. *Instructional Science*, 38, 679–705.

Kiewra, K. (2012). Using graphic organizers to improve teaching and learning. *Idea Paper # 51*. http://theideacenter.org/sites/default/files/idea_paper_51.pdf

Kiewra, K. A. (2005). *Learn how to study and SOAR to success*. Upper Saddle River, NJ: Pearson Prentice Hall.

Lambiotte, J.G., Dansereau, D.F., Cross, D.R., & Reynolds, S.B. (1989). Multirelational semantic maps. *Educational Psychology Review*, 1, 331–367.

Describes features of knowledge maps, and considers both their strengths and weaknesses.

Mickes, L. & Harris C. (2013, January 15). Never forget a Face(book): Memory for online posts beats faces and books. *Science Daily*. Retrieved August 16, 2013, from http://www.sciencedaily.com/ releases/2013/01/130115085841.htm

Mott, M.S., Robinson, D.H., Walden, A., Burnette, J., and Rutherford, A.S. (2012). Illuminating the effects of dynamic lighting on student learning. *SAGE OpenJun*, 2(2) DOI: 10.1177/2158244012445585;

This article discusses the effects of different types of lighting on health and learning.

Ogle, R. (2007). Smart world: Breakthrough creativity and the new science of ideas. Boston: *Harvard Business Review Press*.

Both reach and reciprocity are needed to acquire new learning and make it your own.

Ophir, E., Nass, C. and Wagner, A.D. (August 24, 2009). Cognitive control in media multitaskers. *Proceedings of the National Academy of Sciences*. doi:10.1073/pnas.0903620106

Heavy media multitaskers are more susceptible to interference from irrelevant environmental stimuli and from irrelevant representations in memory. This led to the surprising result that heavy media multitaskers performed worse on a test of task-switching ability, likely due to reduced ability to filter out interference from the irrelevant task set.

Peper, R.J., & Mayer, R.E. (1978). Note-taking as a generative activity. *Journal of Educational Psychology*, 70 (4), 514–522.

Outlines three possible explanations for why note-making affects learning outcomes: 1) increases overall attention and orientation to new material; 2) requires more effort and deeper encoding of the material than does merely reading; 3) requires organizing and "making sense" of the material, which tends to integrate new material to information acquired previously.

Plant cell structure. By LadyofHats (Mariana Ruiz) - Self-made using Adobe Illustrator. (The original edited was also made by me,

Ladyof Hats). Licensed under Public domain via Wikimedia Commons. http://commons.wikimedia.org/wiki/File:Plant_cell_structure_svg .svg#mediaviewer/File:Plant_cell_structure_svg.svg

Qadir, F., Zehra, T., & Khan, I. (2011). Use of concept mapping as a facilitative tool to promote learning in pharmacology. *Journal of the College of Physicians and Surgeons Pakistan*, Vol. 21 (8): 476–481.

Concept mapping was not found beneficial in improving examination grades in Pharmacology.

Sana, F., Weston, T., and Cepeda, N.J. (2013). Laptop multitasking hinders classroom learning for both users and nearby peers. *Computers & Education*, Volume 62, March 2013, 24–31. http://dx.doi.org/10.1016/j.compedu.2012.10.003

Study found that participants who multitasked on a laptop during lecture scored lower on a test compared to those who did not multitask. Participants who were in direct view of a multitasking peer scored lower on a test compared to those who were not.

Science Daily. (2009). Do doodle: Doodling can help memory recall. http://www.sciencedaily.com/releases/2009/02/090226210039.htm

According to a study published today in the journal *Applied Cognitive Psychology*, subjects given a doodling task while listening to a dull phone message had a 29% improved recall compared to their non-doodling counterparts.

Sota, M., Leon, M., & Layng, T.V.J. (2011). Thinking through text comprehension II: Analysis of verbal and investigative repertoires. *The Behavior Analyst Today*, 12, 21–33.

This article on reading comprehension analyzes how reading comprehension can be defined, measured and taught.

Tiemann, P. W., & Markle, S. M. (1990). *Analyzing instructional content: A guide to instruction and evaluation*. Seattle, WA: Morningside Press.

This work has some similarities to Bloom's Taxonomy of Cognitive Objectives, but a major difference is in Tiemann and Markle's emphasis on the learning of concepts.

Review and Self-Test

(WEEK 4)

QUIZ Review and Self-Test

Directions: Mark the number that describes your current system of review and self-test.

Yes / True	Sometimes	No / False	
2	1	0	**1.** I don't have time to review all the material before a test.
2	1	0	**2.** I concentrate on getting the big picture rather than the details.
0	1	2	**3.** I test myself over my notes to make sure I remember the material.
0	1	2	**4.** I review material at least once a week.
0	1	2	**5.** I schedule some time every day for review.
0	1	2	**6.** My notes are very organized.
0	1	2	**7.** I focus my study time on details that I don't remember.

Yes / True	Sometimes	No / False	
0	1	2	**8.** I schedule enough time to do at least two or three reviews of the material before a test.
2	1	0	**9.** Until I take an exam I don't know how well prepared I am. The classroom exam is the first time I've been tested over the material.
0	1	2	**10.** When I get tired of reading and note-making, I switch to reviewing or self-testing.
_____			**Total Score** (Add the numbers circled.)

FEEDBACK on Review and Self-Test

1. A good note format (highly organized and condensed) will streamline the review process so you will have time for several reviews before a test.

2. How often are you asked about the big picture on a multiple-choice exam? Probably not very often. The multiple choice format requires knowledge of details and the differences among them. By just reading, you get the big picture. It's making the notes and reviewing that put the details into your memory.

3. If you answered "Yes, I test myself over my notes" good! We hope your notes are designed to make it easy to test yourself. Self-testing shows you what information needs more review—or that you've mastered the information and can stop reviewing.

4. Repetition is the key to memory. All research on memory shows that repeated reviews are the best way to remember anything.

5. Not only repeated reviews, but spaced intervals between reviews are important. Schedule time for review every day or two.

6. If you answered "Yes, my notes are very organized," excellent! An organized format allows frequent reviews and self-tests.

7. If you answered "Yes, I focus study time on details I don't remember," good for you! You are saving time by focusing on what you've not yet mastered.

8. Repetition is the key to memory. Give yourself a pat on the back if you regularly schedule enough time for multiple reviews before an exam.

9. Don't wait! **Before** the exam is the time to find out what you don't know. By self-testing before the exam, you will know what material needs further review.

10. This is an excellent idea. Varying study activities can help you study for longer periods of time.

SCORE INTERPRETATION Review and Self-Test
0–5 Very good!
6–10 Good, but could use improvement
11–20 Help is on the way! Read this chapter carefully.

)) Repeated Reviews and Practice Questions

You've gone to a lot of trouble to make those terrific notes. The process of making them begins to embed the information in your brain—but it's the repeated reviews and self-tests that make information memorable for the long term. Information must be stored in long-term memory before it can be easily accessed, applied and built upon—and you know how your instructors love to ask questions which require you to *apply* the information you have learned!

What We Know about Memory

Over 100 years ago Hermann Ebbinghaus conducted some of the first research into memory and learning. Studies since that time have consistently found that spaced practice (repeated reviews with some time in between them) is the best way to store information in your long-term memory. The number of repetitions and the time in between those repetitions are two main factors involved in the recall of information. For example, if you wanted to learn all the bones of the head and neck, it would be a mistake to go over them 20 times in one sitting and think you had reviewed enough. You'd remember more if you only reviewed parts of the head and neck two or three times per sitting, at five spaced intervals during the day. It might be only half the number of repetitions, but you'll be more likely to remember the information because of what is called the "spacing effect."

The number of reviews it takes to get information into your long term memory depends on several factors (motivation, prior knowledge, complexity of the material, distractions, etc.) but the general guideline is that easy material that is already somewhat familiar may take only five spaced repetitions, while complex material that you find less engaging may take up to 16 spaced repetitions.

There are two main factors involved in this process. First, you have to have some idea of what the information is (name and location of bones), which you'll get from reviewing. But you also have to be able to access and apply the information. The practice of accessing and applying information is where self-testing comes in. Just because you have reviewed the information repeatedly, does not mean you can access it quickly enough to do well on a test. So remember, there are two parts to effective and efficient

learning: 1) storing the information in your long-term memory and 2) retrieving the information repeatedly, quickly and accurately.

In college, you will typically have three to four major exams for each course. Given that you probably have four or five courses, that means you could have between 12 and 20 exams every semester! How will you be able to review repeatedly? The time frame and number of tests makes it crucial that you stay caught up on your notes, because there is almost always some kind of test coming up soon.

If you are reviewing frequently, you will be eliminating material (by putting it into your "know" pile), which will enable you to focus your time on the material that needs more review (your "don't know" pile). Students often believe that recently presented course material is still fresh in their minds, when actually it may be easier to forget because they have had fewer opportunities to review it.

How many reviews can you fit into the relatively brief period between tests? Ideally, you will be reviewing something every day, sorting your notes into "know" and "don't know" piles and continually adding your new notes as you make them. In the week before an exam you will want to review and self-test on all your notes for that course, including those from the "know" piles, to be sure you have retained the information. You will have encountered portions of the material a number of times:

1. During pre-reading
2. Listening to the lecture
3. Creating rough lecture notes
4. Reading the textbook
5. Looking over class handouts
6. Creating a final set of notes
7. Spaced review
8. Spaced review
9. Self-test
10. Final review of everything before the exam

With this many repetitions, how could you NOT know the information?

Reasons to Self-Test

1. **Be prepared.** Rather than being surprised on test day, why not test yourself in advance, while you still have time to learn the information? Tests tell the teacher how well you have mastered the material, but why wait? You can walk into a test confident that your preparation was thorough by self-testing.

2. **Save time.** Self-testing will tell you where you need to spend your review time. Material that you have mastered will be set aside until the final review, a few days before the exam. This will give you time to focus on less-remembered information.

3. **Simulate the real thing.** No matter how much information is stored in your head, if you can't access it for a test, what good does it do?

4. **Increase motivation and focus attention.** Although it feels good to review material that you have mastered, it is to your

benefit to pay more attention to what you don't know. Spend your time in review of the less familiar material.

How to Review and Self-Test

Quickly read the information on a chart or diagram one or two times. Immediately cover the entire chart except for the outside labels across the top and down the far left column. Write or say the answers to test yourself to see how much of it you remember. That's all there is to it. You should consider the content mastered when you score a 90% or higher on the entire note. The rule for effective reviewing is to do it quickly and frequently.

Taking time to write the answers has two main benefits. 1) It will keep you honest. Once you commit your answer to paper, it is much more difficult to say, "That's what I meant," when you look at the answer and discover that what you have written doesn't match what is in the chart. If they don't match, then you have not yet mastered the information. 2) Writing the answer has a kinesthetic benefit. The act of writing helps embed information in your long-term memory.

Tips for Reviewing and Self-Testing

› Carry flash cards and/or other note types with you every day—paper or digital.

› Each box in a category chart is like a single flash card. If you miss only a few boxed items you can pencil in a small check mark (✓) in that box to remind you that the item needs further review. If, after two or three reviews, you have not learned those details, then make flash cards for those facts. You can also make cards for details you have not learned from flow charts or diagrams.

› Store your charts in file folders or in a binder with tabs labeled "know" and "don't know." Carry a binder or folder with charts to review (instead of a book) when you know you'll have time during the day to review. Create these same folders on your computer and sort the same way (by chapter or topic and "know" or "don't know").

› Sketch out the chart or diagram on a dry erase board to self-test.

› Keep review periods short. We suggest no more than five minutes per chart or diagram. This will allow enough time for repeated reviews at spaced intervals.

› When self-testing from your electronic notes, you can copy the file, delete information in boxes, type answers in boxes and score. Also, research which applications will score and record your practice tests. (Quizlet, Flashcard, ANKI, Study-Blue, etc.)

› Select a corner of your paper chart to keep track of reviews (R) and self-tests (ST) by making tally marks on the charts or diagrams themselves. For example R// means you have reviewed that chart twice and ST 75% means you have self-tested once and scored 75%, which means you have not yet

Chart 4.1   Example of a Review and Self-Test Record

	Definition	Structure / Gap Junction	Function / Speed /Plasticity
Chemical Synapse	Predominant kind Functional connections between neurons &/or other types of cells (muscles / glands) Site of action for majority of psychoactive drugs	Asymmetric in structure Gap junction / nexus junction: cells approach w/in 20–40 nm (called a synaptic cleft)	Post-synaptic potential caused by opening of ion channels by chem. transmitters Produce complex behaviors Slower than elec. delay = 2ms ✓
Electrical Synapse	Mechan & elec. conductive link b'tween 2 neuron cells — gap junction	Gap junction: cells approach w/in 3.5nm ✓ (much closer than chem.)	Direct electrical coupling b'tween neurons Often found in neural systems / retina / cerebral cortex Produce simple, but quick behaviors Faster than chem. delay = 0.2 ms Evidence of plasticity

R=//; //; //
ST=75%; 88%; 100%

mastered the material. The ✓ mark shows the details missed. (See the example above.) Mastery is 90% or better. Most applications will keep track of this for you, but if yours doesn't, you can keep track of your reviews and scores on your phone using the notes function.

When to Schedule Your Review and Self-Test Time

If you are an early riser, do your review first thing in the morning. If you're not, just before dinner is often a good time to schedule a session for review and self-test. The weekend also works well, because you are not getting new information during that time.

You should plan to spend between thirty minutes and an hour per day on reviewing and self-testing. You will spend more

time reviewing and self-testing as the exam approaches, of course. But you will not be in "frantic cramming mode," because you will know you have done a good job of preparing.

Some students find that taping copies of their charts on the bathroom mirror or bedroom closet door can help them use odd bits of time (while brushing teeth, fixing hair or getting dressed) to review important material.

Study Tip: Sleepiness or fatigue during a study period may be a cue that it's time to switch activities. Self-testing will often raise your level of motivation, especially when you find out you don't know some of the material!

Scoring Self-Tests

In order to know how well you have mastered the material, we suggest that you score your self-tests. For example, if you are reviewing a category chart that has five columns and five rows, you will have 25 details to master. When you self-test and miss ten of those items, you may say to yourself, "I knew most of the information." That is correct. You knew 15 out of 25 items. But "most" of the information (15/25) is only 60%. That score is not high enough to pass an exam. You should plan to master 90% of the information that you have in your notes.

Why 90%? Tests are a sample of the content assigned. To increase the odds that your sample of the material matches what the teacher samples on the exam, near complete mastery of your notes will improve your chances of doing well. So measure (score) precisely and aim for 90% mastery of the information.

Using Old Exams to Self-Test

If your professor allows you to have access to old tests (tests used in previous courses that cover the same material) you can also use them as a resource, but don't expect the current exam to be exactly the same. The best way to use an old exam is to actually answer each of the questions, as if it were the real exam. How did you do? The answer to that question will help you pinpoint where you need to focus your additional review and self-testing efforts.

Another strategy for using old exams goes one step further. In addition to choosing the correct answer for each question, you also give the reasons for *not* choosing the other options. This approach will widen your knowledge base and make sure you have a broader understanding of the material.

Act & Analyze
Incorporate Reviewing and Self-Testing into Your Schedule

Exercise 1

You should already have a regular schedule of pre-reading, reading and note-making. Now add in some time on your calendar for review and self-test. Typically about 30 minutes to an hour each day.

Exercise 2

Review one set of flashcards least five times in one day. When you sort them in the evening, you should be able to put most of them into your "know" pile. In the week before an exam, go over all your notes once more. Schedule these review sessions at least 48-hours before the exam. This will give you time to fill in any gaps in your knowledge, without resorting to cramming. If the final exam is comprehensive, that is, over all the material in the course, make sure to review and self-test on *all* your notes in the last week before the final.

Exercise 3

After you have reviewed your charts at least twice, self-test. Keep track of your score next to the ST written on your chart. For example, ST (60%), (75%), (90%).

At the end of the week return to the section below and complete the Check-Up below.

Analyze & Adjust
Check-Up

Incorporate Reviewing and Self-Testing into Your Schedule

1. Did you schedule a time for review and self-test every day? If yes, what time of day worked best for you?

_____

_____

2. Did you carry and sort flashcards (or charts) every day? If so, how many reviews did you average per day?

_____

3. What percentage of the cards or notes went into the "know" pile each day?

_____

⟫ Summary

Congratulations! You have completed the portion of the book that teaches the basic steps of this study system.

The system begins with time management. Through the experiences provided by the time planning and management exercises, you have learned to schedule enough time for the rest of the steps.

The primary components of the study system are:

> Time Planning and Management
> Pre-reading (Preparing for lecture)
> Reading
> Note Making
> Reviewing
> Self-Testing

This system focuses on learning details and storing information in long-term memory. Information must be stored in long-term memory before it can be easily accessed and applied in a meaningful way.

In Steps 5 and 6, Keep Focused and Productive Self-Talk, we will cover ways to enhance this study system. You can achieve even greater success by implementing these additional strategies to maintain motivation and reduce anxiety.

If you want to learn more about self-testing, also called "retrieval practice" and the "testing effect," Karpicke, Roediger, Rohrer and others have done much of the research. Some of their work is listed in the references at the end of this chapter.

Chart 4.2   Six Steps Overview

Study Activity	Time of Day/ Week	Purpose/Rationale	Study Behavior
Preparing for Lecture (Pre-reading)	• Prior to lecture. • Prior to reading.	• Activate prior knowledge. • See the big picture of the topic to be covered. • Increase concentration while reading. • Increase reading speed.	• Scan objectives, summary, bold-faced words, charts, diagrams, study questions. • Watch related videos • Ask yourself, "What is this page about?" or "What main topic is covered in this section?"
Reading and Note-making	• Choose best time of day for high concentration. • Schedule 30-minute to 2-hour blocks.	• Fit details into the big picture. • Understand how to apply principles, if appropriate. • Organize content into easily memorable format. • Make compact, organized notes for review and self-testing	• Concentrate until you clearly understand main topic, principles and/or details. • Make charts. • Make diagrams. • Make cards.
Reviewing	Either first or last study activity— daily.	Increase retention, speed and recall.	Re-read charts, diagrams, cards—any condensed notes.
Self-testing	• After review. • When motivation drops during a study period or as a change from other study activities. • At least twice weekly.	• Increase motivation. • Check on retention. • Determine where further review of specific topics is needed. • Know when you can stop studying.	• Use practice tests. • Sort flash cards. • Cover details in charts and fill in details on another sheet of paper. Ask yourself questions and score the answers. • Sort into "know" and "don't know." Review "don't know" until you reach 90% comprehension.

⟩⟩ References

Clark, R.C. & Lyons, C. (2004). *Graphics for learning*. San Francisco: Pfeiffer.

This book explores the way graphics support the learning process. Research regarding cognitive load, building mental models or schema and the use of matrices or charts is especially pertinent.

Dunlosky, J., Rawson, K.A., Marsh, E.J., Nathan, M.J. and Willingham, D.T. (2013). Improving students' learning with effective learning techniques: Promising directions from cognitive and educational psychology. *Psychological Science in the Public Interest* 14 (1) 4–58, Sage Publications, Inc. DOI: 10.1177/1529100612453266 https://www.wku.edu/senate/documents/improving_student_learning_dunlosky_2013.pdf

Practice testing and distributed practice received high utility assessments because they benefit learners of different ages and abilities and have been shown to boost students' performance across many criterion tasks and in educational contexts.

Farr, M.J. (1987). *The long-term retention of knowledge and skills*. New York: Springer-Verlag.

This book presents a thorough review of the scientific literature on learning, memory and retention, including Ebbinghaus' work originally published in 1885.

Howard, P.J., (2000). *The owner's manual for the brain: Everyday applications from mind-brain research* (2nd ed.). Atlanta, GA: Bard Press.

Chapter 7 is entitled A Good Night's Sleep: Cycles, Dreams, Naps and Nightmares and reviews research of each, including the link between sleep and memory.

Karpicke, J.D. & Blunt, J.R. (2011). Retrieval practice produces more learning than elaborative studying with concept mapping. *Science*, 331, 772–775.
DOI: 10.1126/science.1199327

Karpicke, J.D. & Roediger, H.L., III. (2007). Repeated retrieval during learning is the key to long-term retention. *Journal of Memory and Language* 57, 151–162.
http://learninglab.psych.purdue.edu/downloads/2007_Karpicke_Roediger_JML.pdf

Repeated recall of previously learned items enhanced retention by more than 100%. Repeated retrieval of information is the key to long-term retention.

Kiewra, K. (2012). Using graphic organizers to improve teaching and learning. *Idea Paper #51.*
http://theideacenter.org/sites/default/files/idea_paper_51.pdf

Kiewra, K. A. (2005). *Learn how to study and SOAR to success.* Upper Saddle River, NJ: Pearson Prentice Hall.

Roediger, H. L., III, & Finn, B. (2010). The pluses of getting it wrong. *Scientific American Mind* 21, 38–41.
DOI:10.1038/scientificamericanmind0310-38

Students who take tests on material before studying it remember the information better and longer than those who study without pretesting.

Roediger, H. L., III, Putnam, A. L., & Smith, M. A. (2011). Ten benefits of testing and their applications to educational practice. *Psychology of Learning and Motivation*, 44, 1–36.
http://psych.wustl.edu/memory/Roddy%20article%20PDF's/BC_Roediger%20et%20al%20(2011)_PLM.pdf

Quizzing enables better metacognitive monitoring for both students and teachers because it provides feedback as to how well learning is progressing. Greater learning would occur in educational settings if students used self-testing as a study strategy and were quizzed more frequently in class.

Rohrer, D., Taylor, K., & Sholar, B. (2010). Tests enhance the transfer of learning. *Journal of Experimental Psychology: Learning, Memory, and Cognition*, 36, 233–239.
http://uweb.cas.usf.edu/~drohrer/pdfs/Rohrer_et_al_2010JEPLMC.pdf

An experiment was performed in which two tests were administered to groups of students. One test required exactly the same task seen during the learning session, and the other test consisted of new, more challenging questions. In both experiments, testing effects were found for both kinds of tests, and the testing effect was actually slightly larger for the test requiring transfer.

(**Note:** The testing effect is the ability to learn information more effectively by being tested on it, rather than repeated reading or review.)

Keep Focused

(WEEK 5)

QUIZ Factors Affecting Concentration

Directions: The following statements describe a particular study situation. Indicate how much (or how frequently) each statement applies to your own study style, according to the following scale:

0 = seldom (less than 40% of the time)
1 = sometimes / often (41%–70% of the time)
2 = almost always (71–100% of the time)

Circle the number that best reflects your current study habits.

Seldom/Never	Sometimes/Often	Almost Always	
0	1	2	**1.** As I read and make notes, I tell myself that I am interested in the information.
0	1	2	**2.** I sit at a desk while studying.
0	1	2	**3.** I study in a quiet place.

Seldom/Never	Sometimes/Often	Almost Always		
0	1	2	**4.**	I am able to study for a full hour without taking a break.
0	1	2	**5.**	I am alert and focused while studying.
0	1	2	**6.**	I set a goal for the amount of work I want to get done in each study period.
0	1	2	**7.**	If I begin to feel tired during a study period, I take a brief break to eat a snack or do some quick exercises to boost my energy.
2	1	0	**8.**	I stare out the window or daydream during a study period.
0	1	2	**9.**	I keep a slight sense of urgency or time pressure while studying.
0	1	2	**10.**	My study space is cleared of everything other than the materials I need to study at that time.
0	1	2	**11.**	As I study, I think about how I can use this information in the future.
0	1	2	**12.**	If I catch my thoughts wandering while studying, I easily stop those thoughts and return my attention to my work.
0	1	2	**13.**	I typically study at the same place and at regular times.
0	1	2	**14.**	I am able to quickly begin my work as I start a study session.

SCORE GUIDELINES   Factors Affecting Concentration

There are seven concentration factors to score. It is important for you to know which, if any, of these factors may be a problem for you. Calculate your percentage on each factor by dividing your score by 4. See the example below.

Factor	My Score	Total Possible	My Percentage
Being awake and alert while studying Items 2, 5	2 + 1 = 3 (sum of scores on the two questions)	4	75% (3/4) 75% effective on this factor)

Now you can calculate your score on each of the seven concentration factors and also your overall concentration score.

Seven Factors	My Score	My Percentage (my score divided by 4)
1. Questions about being **awake and alert** during study sessions Add scores of items 2, 5.		
2. Questions about maintaining a **positive mood** while studying. Add scores of items 1, 11.		
3. Questions about avoiding **external distractions.** Add scores of items 3, 10.		
4. Questions about avoiding **internal distractions** (that distract you from your studies). Add scores of items 8, 12.		
5. Questions about maintaining a sense of urgency while studying by **working fast.** Add scores of items 6, 9.		
6. Questions about ability to **study for relatively long periods** of time without stopping. Add scores of items 4, 7.		
7. Questions about **cues in the study environment** that prompt you to start studying. Add scores of items 13, 14.		

SCORE INTERPRETATION

Are you getting the most out of your study time?

Look at the "My Percentage" column. Circle the three lowest percentages. These are the areas that present the most opportunity for improvement. The scores which you circled are the factors to which you should pay most attention in the rest of the chapter.

If your percentage for every factor was consistently at 75% or better, good job! You are typically focused on your work when you study.

If any score under "My Percentage" was lower than 75%, you have identified an area that offers an opportunity for improvement.

Concentrating on your work is a skill that can be learned. Remember, this is a workbook. Doing the practice exercises is what will help you improve.

❱❱ Accomplish More in Less Time

What would you say if someone offered you six extra hours of study time every week? Would you believe it was possible? If you scored lower than 75% on any concentration factor, you can give yourself that gift of time.

Let's do the calculations. Suppose you spend 20 hours a week in personal study (studying on your own, not in class or with a group). If you are concentrating only 50% of that time, you are wasting at least ten whole hours every week! If you can raise your level of concentration by even 10%, you can gain two more hours. If you can get your level of concentration up to 80%, you will recapture six hours each and every week. Over a 15-week semester, that would add up to 90 additional hours of study! Think how much extra review you could gain with that 90 extra hours to study! Or, seen the other way, wouldn't it be great to have that many hours freed up for other activities, because you were more efficient in your work?

Interruptions—Scheduled and Unscheduled

A scheduled or planned interruption is called a break. Because of the daily rhythms we all go through, it's best not to go longer than two hours without taking a physical break from your studies. Remember the ultradian rhythms discussed in the introduction to this book? Our bodies will let us know when we need a break. According to Dr. Ernest Rossi, in his book *The 20-Minute Break,* here are some cues to watch for:

> Feeling a need to stretch

> Yawning or sighing

> Finding yourself hesitating or procrastinating

> Noticing your body getting tense or fatigued

> Feeling hungry

> Mind wandering

> Making careless errors

Unscheduled interruptions are likely to come from friends and family stopping by for a visit or checking in with a call or a text. By their very nature, unplanned interruptions are harder to control. But because interruptions are likely to occur, you can plan how you're going to deal with them before they happen.

Interruptions quickly devour time and concentration. Researchers have found that even short interruptions can impair your concentration for up to six minutes. And if it's a long interruption or takes place at the beginning of a study period, it can take up to 20 minutes to fully regain your previous level of concentration.

We suggest you experiment with various apps that deal with focus and concentration (Pomodoro, FocusTime, 30/30, etc.), but realize that you may have to join the many other students who turn off their phones and store them out of sight while trying to fully concentrate.

While taking an online course, or completing an online assignment, if you find other sites to be a distraction, devise a system or install an application that will prevent your visiting sites unrelated to your studies during that time.

Act & Analyze
Exercises for the Seven Factors Affecting Concentration

Factor 1—Awake and Alert

When you feel wide awake and alert for important information, you obviously can learn more in less time. If you are sleepy, or hungry, or restless, it's hard to concentrate on any task. Adequate sleep, good nutrition and exercise are the first steps to efficient study. You need at least seven and a half to nine hours of sleep each night. You need to eat two or preferably three meals and a maybe a couple of snacks a day and get some regular exercise.

When you study, put your work in the center of your desk or study table, directly under a good light. If you're using your computer, make sure the monitor and keyboard are at the correct heights and angles. Your posture should be telling you that you are awake and alert. Sit in a back-supporting chair. Do not recline in an armchair or on a bed or sofa. Lying down suggests to your body (and your brain) that it is time for rest or sleep. Your posture tells you that you are ready to work—or not.

Making notes while you study is a good way to stay alert and it is difficult to make notes while reclining.

Exercise 1

Set a timer for ten-minute intervals. Whenever the timer sounds, check your posture. Is your back straight? Are your eyes in line with your study materials? Is your computer screen adjusted correctly? Are your feet flat on the floor? Do this exercise daily until your body is always in the awake and alert position when you are studying.

Exercise 2

To maintain your energy during a study period, prepare easy-to-eat snacks, such as vegetable sticks, crackers, nuts, cheese or fruits. These snacks don't take much time to prepare and they will keep up your energy while you study. Don't take more than ten minutes to consume your snacks during each hour of study. Recall from Step 1 that you must study at least 50 minutes of every hour to count an hour of study.

Exercise 3

When you notice that your attention begins to lag, but it's not yet time for a break, switch study activities. You can do some pre-reading for the next day's lecture. Or, to really rouse yourself, self-test over material you previously studied. Self-testing is highly motivating, especially if you find you can't remember some important information. A little anxiety can be a big wake-up call. Use your notes and charts, materials from your teacher, book or online resources for self-testing. Put aside whatever you were doing when you got sleepy and completely switch to another study activity.

Exercise 4

If you're feeling drowsy, take a 10–15-minute break for physical exercise to get your blood going. You don't need a gym or special equipment to do toe touches, push-ups, jumping jacks, squats or

stretches. Turn on some music and dance! Again, no more than 10–15 minutes before you're back at work with more oxygen in your brain.

Factor 2—Productive Attitude

Encourage yourself. It's hard to work well when you don't feel good about what you're doing. If you're thinking, "I can't control what I think or how I feel," think again! You can control your mood by controlling what you think. Emotions are the result of thoughts, and you are, or should be, in charge of your own thoughts. Read Step 6 about productive self-talk very carefully.

Here are some examples of internal messages (thoughts, feelings) that *get in the way* of productive studying:

I wish I could be with my friends instead of having to study.
I'll never learn all this stuff.
I'll never need to know any of this in real life.

Here are some examples of internal messages that *help you stay focused* on your studies:

This information will be useful, not only for the test but maybe in other ways.

I am lucky to be able to go to college.
It will feel good to have learned this information.

Here are three suggestions for increasing your productive thinking when studying. Tell yourself your studies are:

> **Interesting.** If you really want to be a successful college student, what you are learning *should* be interesting, because you will need to know it to do well in your classes and perhaps in your future career.

> **Useful.** Say to yourself, "I need to know this in order to do well in this course."

> Will help you **achieve your goal.** To achieve your goal of graduation, you need to pass each class and maintain a good grade point average. Imagine yourself performing well on the next test.

Some students recently told us that they use the "game show question" strategy on themselves when they don't see the current relevance of something they are studying. They say, "This could be the winning question someday when I am on 'Jeopardy,' so if I learn it now, this information could help me win a million dollars in the future!"

Exercise 1

Have you ever noticed how some elite athletes take a moment to "psych up" just as they are about to perform? They are mentally preparing themselves by envisioning success. Before each study session during the next week, take a moment to say something motivating about learning the material you plan to study. By "psyching up" at the beginning of each study session, you put yourself in a good frame of mind to concentrate and learn.

Here are some suggestions for motivating thoughts as you start your study session:

I want to learn all I can about this so I can do well in class and on the exam.
This topic could be important to me later.
I am going to try to figure out what other people (like our teacher) think is so interesting about this topic.

Factor 3—External Distractions

In the chapter on time management, we suggested that sometimes you can save time by doing two things at once, if neither requires all your attention. For example, listening to music while exercising. This time-saving tip definitely does not apply to studying. **Don't try to do anything else while studying.** Recent research on multitasking indicates that when people try to do more than one (serious) task at a time, they make more mistakes.

To improve your concentration, turn off all background noise. Students sometimes claim that background music or TV helps them study. Ask yourself, "If I am listening to the music at any level at all, is not some part of my brain distracted away from my studies?" Whether it is the television or music, some part of your brain is paying attention to it. In fact, research indicates that

External distractions decrease your ability to focus.

multi-tasking slows you down and increases the chance of making mistakes in your work. It seems the lateral frontal and pre-frontal cortex and possibly the superior frontal cortex cannot process two tasks at once. So turn off the TV and music until it's time to take a break. The single exception to this rule is for those diagnosed with ADHD. A few studies indicate that they may benefit from listening to instrumental music while they study. The study was not conclusive, however, so don't use that as an excuse to crank up the music.

If you still choose to listen to music while you study, even though you now know it lessens your ability to concentrate, here are a couple of guidelines to make it a bit less of a distraction and less fatiguing:

> Instrumental music only. Listening to one set of words (lyrics) while reading a different set of words (from your study materials) is extremely fatiguing for your brain.

> Do not use ear buds. Using ear buds physically stimulates the nerve endings in your ears and makes it difficult for your brain to ignore the music. If the music is playing in the background, your brain can more easily choose to listen—or not.

Your study area itself may be distracting. Do not place your study desk or table near a window where you can see what is going on outdoors. You do not want a view to pull your eyes away from your study materials. Also, remove any souvenirs, photographs, even text books from other classes. Clear off anything that might take your thoughts away from your current topic of study.

Exercise 1

Go to your study space. Look at everything on the work surface and everything you can see while you are studying. How many of these objects do you actually need for your upcoming study session? How much can you see that might distract your mind from the materials you intend to study? Remove those objects and put them out of the line of sight.

What is the one thing you should add to your study area to make it more effective? This is a trick question. The answer is, "nothing." It is more likely that you will have to remove objects from your study area in order to concentrate better. Clear away anything you will not be studying during a particular session. The only objects you need for your study session are a desk or table, chair, light, and your study materials for one class. Nearby, out of your line of vision, you can store materials for other classes.

Exercise 2

Now that the top of your desk or table is clear, look around the rest of the area. Make it difficult to see anything but what you are studying at that moment. Put your desk or work table facing a blank wall. Have a storage place (book shelf, cabinet) with your books and supplies from all your classes nearby but out of sight. Being reminded of other subjects you need to study may cause you to vacillate between your current study topic and some other topic you plan to study at a different time.

Have a strong light directly over your study materials. If you are easily distracted, it may help to turn off other lights in the room and leave only the bright light over your workspace. The focus of the light serves to draw attention only where it is shining.

Exercise 3

When you are working at a computer, stronger light is probably not the best option. Adjust the brightness, angle and height of the monitor so the screen is easy to see, with no glare from lights or windows. The top of the monitor should be level with your eyes and you should be seated about an arm's length away. Remember the 20/20/20 rule: every 20 minutes take a 20-second break and look at least 20 feet away. Looking at something far away every few minutes helps relieve and prevent eye strain.

Factor 4—Internal Distractions

Internal distractions can be pleasant or unpleasant. Happy internal distractions might include wishing you were at the beach with a special friend or thinking about what to wear to an upcoming event. Frequently, though, internal distractions are less pleasant.

Worry is enormously distracting. Students often have much to worry about besides studies: relationships, family issues and financial concerns. You are probably in the age-range when it is natural to be thinking about relationships. Your parents may be facing issues of employment or aging, which could also cause worrisome thoughts.

A student once said he had difficulty concentrating while studying at his desk, because his thoughts kept going to his financial concerns. Some exploration revealed that his financial worries were being cued by a stack of unpaid bills that he kept in a basket on the corner of his desk. Whenever his eyes wandered over to that spot, his thoughts quite naturally shifted away from his studies and toward his debts. Once he placed the bills in a desk drawer, his ability to concentrate improved dramatically. If you are plagued with internal distractions, the following exercises may help.

Exercise 1

Keep a note card or a scrap of paper to record straying thoughts. Each time you catch your thoughts wandering away from your studies, write down the subject of your wandering thoughts. Is there a pattern? Look for cues near your study area that might be causing your thoughts to stray. For this particular exercise it's better to use paper than the notes function on your phone. Picking up your phone may cause an additional distraction.

Exercise 2

Silly as it sounds, this exercise works. If your stray thoughts show a persistent pattern of worry, get out your schedule and set a specific time to deal with the problem. If it is a problem that you can resolve, take care of it at the scheduled time. If it's worrying about something over which you have no control (all too often the case), schedule the time anyway. Tell yourself you'll worry about it at the scheduled time and get back to your studies. Then absolutely follow through on your plan to worry at the scheduled time.

We think you'll have a hard time worrying on schedule, but go ahead and try anyway. You will have accomplished two important things: 1) Knowing you have set aside the time to think about the problem lets you get back to your studying; 2) If you discover you can't really worry on schedule, you will have learned from experience the futility of worrying about something over which you have no control.

Exercise 3

Unwanted thoughts creep up on you unconsciously. Your mind may have been off someplace else for ten minutes when you meant to be studying. Watch out for unwanted or straying thoughts and zap them as soon as you become aware that your attention has wandered. One student wore a rubber band on her wrist and gave it a small "pop" the instant she realized her thoughts had drifted to a persistent problem. The zap from the rubber band immediately gave her a slight punishment for wasting time by not concentrating on her studies. If you use this technique, don't pop the rubber band so hard that you hurt yourself, just enough to remind you to keep focused on your work.

Other students have used the word "focus" as a mantra, saying it aloud from time to time, to regain their attention during a study period. See which one works for you.

Exercise 4

You can also argue yourself out of wasting study time. As soon as you catch yourself daydreaming or worrying or whatever you do when you stop thinking about your work, put your study materials to one side. On a piece of scratch paper or a note card, write down what you were doing (daydreaming, worrying, etc.). Then write down, or say, all the reasons why you should not be doing that (waste of time, keep from studying, useless, etc.) Give yourself counter-arguments about the disruptive thought. Remind yourself that your study time is sacred. Return to your studies only when you are certain that your thoughts are under control and you are ready to concentrate on your work.

Exercise 5

Try reading aloud. This is slower than reading silently, but if you will read with emotion and make it interesting to hear, you may gain in understanding what you lose by reading more slowly. Plus, you have the added benefit of not only seeing the information, but also hearing it! You can increase the benefit even more by summarizing in your own words what you have just read aloud because we tend to remember informal language better than formal language (Mickes & Harris, 2013).

Factor 5—Work Pace

It may sound counter-intuitive, but keeping up a quick pace as you study helps your concentration. You may be thinking, "No way! How can I really think about what I'm studying if I'm rushed?" True, there will be occasions when you really have to ponder the material you're studying, for example, understanding how a particular mathematical equation works. Obviously, you should slow down at that point.

Why does keeping up a quick pace help concentration? Because working quickly focuses attention on the task at hand

and does not permit straying thoughts. If you have learned how to speed read, you will know that you cannot think of anything but what you're reading when you read with a sense of urgency. Urgency makes the job more exciting. It's almost impossible to feel bored when you are working as fast as you can.

Exercise 1

Use a timer for this exercise. As you begin your next study session, decide how quickly you want to accomplish each task. Here's an example: in a two-hour evening session, you may decide first to pre-read for fifteen minutes for tomorrow's lecture in geology and then spend one hour and 45 minutes reading and making notes for today's lecture in psychology. After you have completed the pre-reading, time yourself as you read one page of your psychology book. Multiply the number of pages to be read by the number of minutes it took to read one page to decide how many pages you can finish in the allotted time. As an example, if you can read one page in five minutes, see if you can get through twelve pages in one hour. Then you have 45 minutes to make notes on those twelve pages. It's amazing how much a deadline focuses your attention on your work.

Exercise 2

During your next study period, set a timer for 5–10 minutes. As you read, use a straight edge (like a ruler or a note-card) to cover the text you have just read and keep moving it down the page at a steady rate. This technique will help force your eyes down the page. By covering up what you just read, you will be less tempted to re-read. Check the timer periodically to be sure you are completing the tasks on time. You definitely won't be daydreaming or dozing.

Factor 6—Study for Extended Periods

College students are usually able to sit and study for a couple hours at a time. Endurance for concentrating on study materials is a learned ability and improves with practice. It also helps to vary your study method during a long session of concentrated study. For example, during an extended evening study session, you could begin with fifteen minutes of pre-reading for tomorrow. Then you could read and make notes over material presented in today's lectures. Finally, you could do a review over some notes you made yesterday. Or, to raise your motivation, you could insert a short self-test in the middle of a long reading and note-making session.

An interesting biological aspect of scheduling two-hour study sessions comes from the research on ultradian rhythms. These are natural hormonal fluctuations that occur every 90–120 minutes day and night in both men and women. Between each of these 90–120 minute periods of maximum wakefulness and concentration, there are 15–20 minute "troughs" where it is difficult to assimilate new information. That's the ideal time for a break.

Exercise 1

If you have not yet mastered studying in one-hour blocks, challenge yourself to increase your endurance for longer periods of study. Try to extend your regular study time by 15 minutes. After a week, add another 15 minutes to a study session. Within a few weeks you should be able to study for two to three hours with only one or two breaks.

But don't go overboard! After three to four hours of concentrated study you will need a longer break—perhaps as long as an hour—to be refreshed. Even elite athletes and musicians limit intensive practice to a total of four to six hours per day.

Exercise 2

Reward yourself at the end of a long study session. Look over how much you have accomplished and tell yourself how pleased you are to have done so much. Congratulate yourself on how much you have learned. Take a break and know that you deserve it.

Factor 7—Cues to Start Studying or Time-to-Study Rituals

Have you ever heard the saying, "Well begun is half done"? The Greek philosopher Aristotle said that over 2000 years ago.

Getting off to a good start is a real time saver, so this section will discuss ways to dive right in to your work. Study cues can be places, times, or objects. This is why we say that you should not study while lying down on a bed or sofa. Beds and sofas are cues for rest and relaxation, exactly what you do *not* want to do when you are studying. We recommend that you have a special place to study at home and also a particular place or two where you always study at school, for example, a library carrel. The place, if you often study there, is in itself a cue for studying.

Activities can also provide cues to what will follow. Most people have a "getting ready for bed" routine, such as, brushing teeth, face washing, putting on pajamas, setting an alarm, etc. "Time to study" rituals could include: clearing your study area, getting out study materials, positioning the desk lamp, turning off your cell phone, etc. One student told us she removes her jewelry and pulls her hair back. These are cues she uses to tell herself it's "time to get to work."

Time can also cue an activity. If you look at a clock and see that it's noon, you're likely to think, "I need to get some lunch." As far as possible, use the power of cues of specific times and places to get you quickly into your studies. For example, if you regularly study between 7:30 p.m. and 10 p.m. at your special study desk or table, you will find that you can immediately settle into your study session when you sit down there at 7:30 p.m. The place and the time combine to form a powerful cue to get involved in your work quickly.

Exercise 1

If you don't already have one, set up a special place to study at home, preferably where you do nothing else but study. It may not be possible to have a separate study area if you live in a dorm, but the simpler the set-up, the better. You need nothing but a desk or table, a chair and a lamp, preferably with the desk or table facing the wall. We know it sounds boring, but if you are fully concentrating while you're studying, you'll have more time later to get out and have some fun!

If noise is a distraction while you are studying, some options are to: 1) find someplace else to study; 2) use ear plugs or headphones—headphones don't even have to be turned on, they can just muffle the sound; 3) use a white noise generator in the background, like a fan or a white noise app on your phone or computer.

Exercise 2

Find a spot (or two) at school where you can regularly study. The library is an obvious choice, but you may also find a quiet place in a cafeteria or a classroom that is not being used at the specific times you want to study, perhaps when you have an hour or two between lectures. Look around the school at those times to see what place would be available and quiet. Then study at that place regularly. If you can find two possible locations, even better! If one is in use, you'll still have another study spot.

Act & Analyze
Concentration Monitoring

In your study time and in your play time, practice being fully present and engaged. Research by Jon Kabat-Zinn and others indicates that practicing mindfulness will increase your ability to focus and help you enjoy your breaks more!

In each of the boxes in the following chart, estimate your level of concentration as a percentage of your study time spent fully focused on your work for the next week.

Chart 5.1   Concentration Monitoring

	Time:	Time:	Time:
	Morning Study Session	**Aternoon Study Session**	**Evening Study Session**
Monday	%	%	%
Tuesday	%	%	%
Wednesday	%	%	%
Thursday	%	%	%
Friday	%	%	%
Saturday	%	%	%
Sunday	%	%	%

There are also applications available to help you track this. If you find one that works well for you, please let us know.

Analyze & Adjust
Check-up
Concentration Monitoring Exercise

After monitoring your concentration for one week, answer the following questions.

1. Do you see a pattern in your levels of concentration? When is your concentration best? When is it more difficult to concentrate?

_____

_____

_____

2. Can you identify the reason why your concentration was lower during certain study sessions? Which of the seven concentration factors could have been related to this drop in concentration?

_____

_____

_____

3. What do you need to do to improve your ability to focus at those times or places?

_____

_____

_____

Checklist 5.1   Study Area

Your study area *should* include the following elements:

☐ Desk or table

☐ Lamp or good overhead lighting

☐ Chair that promotes good posture

☐ Only the materials for the one subject you are studying

☐ Computer, if needed (monitor & keyboard at correct height)

☐ Comfortable temperature (too warm and you'll go to sleep)

Your study area should *not* include:

☐ Pictures of loved ones

☐ Other study materials (nothing on the desk except what you are studying at that moment)

☐ Bills or other financial statements

☐ An inviting view of the out-of-doors

☐ Anything that cues you to think of something besides the topic you are studying

Checklist 5.2 Before a Study Period

I plan to study from _____ to _____ with a break from _____ to _____.

☐ I know exactly what topics and pages I need to study/learn. They are: _____

_____

☐ I have the resources I need

- Book
- Syllabus
- Computer
- Internet connection
- Study area
- Paper, pens, pencils, markers
- Time
- Study calendar/schedule
- _____

☐ Consequences are in place for each study period.

- If I have a productive study period I will _____

_____

- If I do *not* have a productive study period I will _____

_____

☐ I define a productive study period as _____

_____

☐ I will know I have mastered the information when _____

_____

☐ I have the vocabulary and/or foundational knowledge to be able to understand:

- Lectures
- Reading assignments
- Class discussions

The Roles of Sleep and Nutrition in Cognitive Functioning

Because different types of learning take place during different phases of sleep, a full night's rest (7.5 to 9 hours) every night is an important part of a good study system. Good sleep hygiene includes: sleeping in a cool room (68 degrees Fahrenheit + or − 2 degrees is considered ideal); sleeping in total darkness; going to bed before midnight; and turning off lighted devices (TV, phone, computer, tablet) at least 30 minutes before going to bed.

If you are thinking a lack of sleep is no big deal, Sejnowski & Destexhe (2000), Wulff, Gatti, Wettstein & Foster (2010) and others have written about their findings linking sleep loss to impaired cognition and even psychiatric disorders. See the references section at the end of this chapter for those and other annotated references.

Good nutrition includes eating whole, unprocessed foods, drinking plenty of water, getting adequate protein, healthy fats and limiting sugar or other empty calories. One student said, "I realized that if I have to read the label to see what's in it, I probably shouldn't be eating it!" The vitamin pathways you learn about in biology can't begin the process without your consuming the whole foods that provide the needed nutrients.

Eating sugar or other "fast" or high-glycemic carbohydrates will cause a spike in blood sugar levels. Typically you feel really good for a few minutes, then as blood sugar levels rapidly fall, you "crash" and feel very tired, sleepy and sluggish. Research on how food affects insulin levels says that if you will eat protein or fat along with high-glycemic carbs, you will have less of a rapid rise and descent of your blood sugar levels. So, foods that help you stay alert and focused are foods that help you maintain optimal insulin levels.

)) Summary

↑ Concentration = ↑ Comprehension + ↓ Study Time!

Students get used to many distractions in their study environment and are often surprised to find how much time they can
save when they eliminate disruptions and raise their level of concentration. Focusing on the work in front of you will save time
for all the rest of your busy life. Learn which of the seven concentration factors most affects your ability to focus and use that
information to increase your level of concentration.

Before   After

)) References

Challem, J. (2014). *The Nutrition Reporter.*
Retrieved from www.nutritionreporter.com

Monthly review of clinical research on vitamin, mineral and food
therapies.

Dux, P.E., Invanoff, J., Asplund, C.L. & Marois, R. (2006). Isolation of a
central bottleneck of information processing with time-resolved
fMRI. *Neuron, 52,* 1109–1120.

Research on the effects of multi-taking. There appears to be a
central bottleneck in the brain that prevents us from being able to
do two things at once.

Egoscue, P. (1988). *Pain free: A revolutionary method for stopping chronic pain.* New York: Bantam Books.

Stretches to help relieve and prevent chronic pain. Also: *Pain free at your PC.*

Gibbs, J.J. (1990). *Dancing with your books: The Zen way of studying.* New York: Penguin Books.

Presents Zen methods of increasing concentration while you study.

Kabat-Zinn, J. (2014). Mindfulness based stress reduction. Retrieved from: http://www.mindfullivingprograms.com/whatMBSR.php

Maquet, P. (2001). The role of sleep in learning and memory. *Science,* 294, 1048. http://www.nhhs.net/ourpages/auto/2007/10/29/1193690123726 /sleep%20paper.pdf

Mednick, S.C., & Ehrman, M. (2006). *Take a nap! Change your life.* New York: Workman Publishing.

This book discusses the research on the benefits of napping and shows you how to plan the optimum nap to increase alertness, strengthen memory and reduce stress.

Mickes, L. & Harris C. (2013, January 15). Never forget a Face(book): Memory for online posts beats faces and books. Science Daily. Retrieved August 16, 2013, from http://www.sciencedaily.com /releases/2013/01/130115085841.htm

Occupational Safety and Health Administration. (2014). U.S. Department of Labor. Computer Workstations. https://www.osha.gov/SLTC/etools/computerworkstations /components_monitors.html

Oetting, E. (1964). Hypnosis and concentration in study. *American Journal of Clinical Hypnosis, 7,* 148–151.

Research study shows hypnosis can improve study concentration. This article gives examples of hypnotic suggestions that students could use.

Ophir, E., Nass, C. and Wagner, A.D. (August 24, 2009). Cognitive control in media multitaskers. *Proceedings of the National Academy of Sciences.* doi:10.1073/pnas.0903620106

Heavy media multitaskers are more susceptible to interference from irrelevant environmental stimuli and from irrelevant representations in memory. This led to the surprising result that heavy media multitaskers performed worse on a test of task-switching ability, likely due to reduced ability to filter out interference from the irrelevant task set.

Rosen, L.D., Carrier, L.M., & Cheever, N.A. (2013). Facebook and texting made me do it: Media-induced task-switching while studying. *Computers in Human Behavior,* 29, 948–958. http://drlarryrosen.com/research/published-work/

Students with relatively high use of study strategies were more likely to stay on-task than other students. The educational implications include allowing students short "technology breaks" to reduce distractions and teaching students metacognitive strategies regarding when interruptions negatively impact learning.

Rossi, E.L. (1991). *The 20 minute break: Reduce stress, maximize performance, and improve health and emotional well-being using the new science of ultradian rhythms.* Los Angeles: Jeremy P. Tarcher, Inc.

How our daily ultradian rhythms affect levels of concentration and well-being.

Sana, F., Weston, T., and Cepeda, N.J. (2013). Laptop multitasking hinders classroom learning for both users and nearby peers. *Computers & Education,* Volume 62, March 2013, 24–31. http://dx.doi.org/10.1016/j.compedu.2012.10.003

This study found that participants who multitasked on a laptop during a lecture scored lower on a test compared to those who did not multitask. Participants who were in direct view of a multitasking peer scored lower on a test compared to those who were not.

Schwartz, T., McCarthy, C. & Gomes, J. (2010). *Be excellent at anything: Four changes to get more out of work and life.* NY: Free Press.

One of the suggested changes is getting more sleep at night which leads to being more focused, positive and productive during the day.

Sejnowski T.J. & Destexhe A. (2000, December 15). Why do we sleep? *Brain Research.* 886(1-2):208–223. http://www.unic.cnrs-gif.fr/site_media/pdf/8EAC4FDDd01.pdf

Memories are consolidated while we sleep, by recalling and storing information.

Wark, D.M. (2013). Alert Hypnosis. Presented at the Child Hypnosis Congress, Heidelberg, Oct 31–Nov 3, 2013. Retrieved from: https://cx-services.com/htx12/projects/kindertagung2013 /download/catalogitems/w091/w091-wark.pdf

Suggestions on how to use Alert Hypnosis to increase concentration and comprehension while reading and studying.

Wulff K., Gatti S., Wettstein J.G., Foster R.G. (2010, August). Sleep and circadian rhythm disruption in psychiatric and neurodegenerative disease. *Nature Reviews Neuroscience,* 11(8):589–99. doi: 10.1038/ nrn2868. Epub 2010 Jul 14.

"Disruption of sleep alters sleep-wake timing, destabilizes physiology and promotes a range of pathologies from cognitive to metabolic defects."

Self-Talk

(WEEK 6)

QUIZ Self-Talk

Below are thoughts some students report they have while preparing for or during a test. Indicate how often you might have any of them by circling the appropriate number to the left of each statement.

Almost Always	Sometimes/Often	Seldom/Never	
2	1	0	**1.** "I must get a perfect score on every test."
2	1	0	**2.** "I am dumb."
2	1	0	**3.** "There is too much information. I can't remember it all."
2	1	0	**4.** "I have no future if I fail this test."
2	1	0	**5.** "Why can't this be easier? Why does my life have to be so hard?"

Almost Always	Sometimes/Often	Seldom/Never	
2	1	0	**6.** As I take the test, I keep thinking about the items I have already missed.
2	1	0	**7.** I look at the other students taking the test and think they are probably doing better than me.
2	1	0	**8.** My first reaction to reading a difficult item is 'I can not do this!'
2	1	0	**9.** I worry about what others will think of me when they find out how I did on the test.
2	1	0	**10.** I keep thinking "I am not going to pass."
_____			**Total Score** (Add the numbers circled.)

SCORE INTERPRETATION Self-Talk

> Congratulations if your score was *less than 6 points*. You are not your own worst enemy while preparing for, or during, a test. Good for you!

> If your total was 7–14 complete this chapter carefully.

> If your score was 15 or higher, personal counseling (perhaps at your school counseling center) is also recommended. You will be a happier, more productive person when you stop making yourself miserable with negative and unproductive thoughts.

⟩⟩ What Is Anxiety?

Anxiety is a feeling of fear, which can have emotional, cognitive and physical symptoms. Typically, the greater the sense of threat, the more serious the symptoms.

For most students, the levels of anxiety are in the mild to moderate range, but they can still cause problems. People can become more irritable, angry, sad, withdrawn or apathetic. They may lose concentration, be more easily distracted, remember less or use poor judgment. They may experience different levels of the "fight, flight or freeze" syndrome, including rapid heart rate, perspiration, faster breathing and muscular tension. Our bodies have learned to deal with a threat by physical effort—either running away or fighting the enemy. But how can we deal with our modern stressors?

Decisions about what is threatening occur in the frontal cortex of the brain. Your brain decides what poses a threat and the responses follow. It all begins with your perception of threat. The physical responses follow that thought.

Motivation and Difficult Tasks

We need motivation when faced with difficult tasks, but let's not confuse motivation (moderate increase in the fight or flight response) with debilitating anxiety or fear.

If there is little or no motivation, performance is low. As motivation increases, so does performance—up to a point. When motivation becomes extreme anxiety, performance begins to decrease. In his book *Overachievement*, John Eliot says,

> . . . arousal and anxiety are not the same thing. You simply have been conditioned or taught to treat them as equals. They're not.
>
> • The physical symptoms of fight or flight are what the human body has learned over thousands of years to operate more efficiently and at the highest level.
>
> • Anxiety is a cognitive *interpretation* of that physical response. (p 25)

Figure 6.1   Motivation Curve

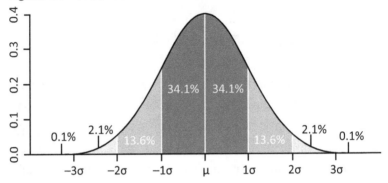

Based on Image provided by Wikipedia. http://en.wikipedia.org/wiki/Normal_distribution#mediaviewer
/File:Standard_deviation_diagram.svg

Test Anxiety

Some students may see tests as a threat. After all, you must at least pass it, or there will be unpleasant consequences. It is sometimes hard to know whether that perception is realistic (the student knows he or she has not studied enough) or unrealistic, based on incorrect or dysfunctional thinking. The results are the same in either case. The over-anxious student is highly distractible, nervous and has difficulty focusing on review materials prior to the test and on test questions during the test. The student whose motivation is within reasonable bounds is able to concentrate on the task at hand.

Most people are more aware of their physical symptoms of anxiety than they are of the thoughts that cause them. It is, however, much more efficient to attack the root causes of anxiety—your thoughts—than to work on the physical symptoms. The trick is to identify negative thoughts before they have a chance to put your body on red alert, and to replace them with more productive thoughts.

If you have difficulty controlling the physical symptoms of anxiety, your counseling center may offer a session in reducing anxiety. If it's not offered to groups, you may be able to get individual counseling.

Changing the Way You Think

Good news! Controlling negative thinking is just like getting control of any other behavior. Negative or unproductive thinking patterns are often just bad habits. True, you have probably learned them over a lifetime, so they are rather deeply embedded habits. But they are learned behaviors. Since you learned them, you can also unlearn them and replace unproductive thoughts with more productive thoughts. You *can* change a bad attitude and possibly even learn to look forward to academic challenges.

The following chart outlines the seven main types of negative, unproductive thoughts and their possible consequence.

If any of these types of negative thoughts are hanging around in your head, you will not be working at your best while studying or taking a test. Imagine trying to concentrate on reviewing your notes while part of your brain is saying, "Why try? You're a loser."

Saying, "I can't stand it" to yourself keeps you from persisting in the task. It's easier to give up if you feel a little frustrated or tired and go watch a movie or call a friend. It's also sometimes a reason students leave tests early, before they have a chance to review their answers and make sure they have not made any careless errors. They think, "I can't stand this one more minute. Get me out of here."

If you think the task is overwhelming ("It's driving me crazy!"), you could be justified in doing anything else, even least favorite tasks like dish-washing and vacuum-cleaning, to avoid it.

Perhaps inevitable doom is the worst of them. The student goes from, "I don't know if I'll remember this factoid on the test," to "then I'll flunk the test," to "then I'll fail the course," to "then I'll be expelled from school," to "then my life will be ruined!" These thoughts can occur at the speed of light. You aren't even aware of how you got from, "Will I remember?" to "My life is ruined!"

A champion negative thinker can use all seven types of negative thoughts, but most of us stick with one or two favorite kinds. And all this is below the level of consciousness.

Table 6.1   Seven Types of Unproductive Thoughts

	Unproductive Thoughts	Possible Consequences
1	If I am not perfect, I am a *total loser*. There is nothing in between being on the top rung of perfection and the absolute bottom of the ladder in life. I must always fight for the top position.	Anxiety, lack of focus, making careless errors due to worrying
2	I am *helpless* to do anything about my situation. My life is totally controlled by outside forces. I can do nothing to help myself. I am no good at (fill in the blank).	Depression, tendency to give up, failure to keep working on the task
3	I'm *not good enough*. I will never succeed. Any failure only confirms my fundamental belief in my own worthlessness. I can't understand how I got into college. They must have mixed up the applications in the admissions office. I don't belong here.	Depression, tendency to give up, tiredness
4	Other *people are bad*. Other people cause all my problems. Any problem I have is all the fault of someone else. They are out to get me!	Anger, complaining, friends avoid spending time with you
5	*I can't stand it*. It is awful. It is unbearable. It'll kill me (whatever it is).	Fear, avoiding the task
6	*If only* . . . I were a prince or princess and had a fairy godmother. Things should be better or easier for me. Why should life be so hard for me?	Lethargy, day-dreaming, wasted time, loss of concentration
7	*I am doomed*. A bad fairy presided over my birth and now my life is cursed. I'll never be lucky. Sooner or later, some terrible thing is going to happen to me. Nothing will ever go right. There is nothing I can do to change my horrible fate. I'll never achieve my goals. Why even try?	Depression, dread, chronic worry, distraction

Are You Ready to Make a Change?

The steps in stopping negative, unproductive thinking are:

A. Identify the situation (e.g., taking a test) in which the negative thought occurs.

B. Identify the underlying thought ("I'm going to fail"). This is sometimes hard at first but gets easier with practice.

C. Notice the consequence of your negative thought (e.g., you stop concentrating, start perspiring, etc.).

Act & Analyze

Exercise 1
Learn to Identify Unproductive Thoughts

In each of the following scenarios, the **situation** (A) is identified for you, as is the emotional, physical, or behavioral **consequence** (C) of the negative thought. Your task is to write in the blank what negative thought or **belief** (B) might logically fit in that sequence.

1. A. Situation: Lynn is sitting in lecture, and the student sitting in the next seat turns with a smile and asks, "Are you ready for the test tomorrow?"
   B. Belief/Thought: Lynn thinks_____

   _____

   C. Consequence: Lynn squirms, tenses, swallows, looks away and takes a long time to respond.

2. A. Situation: Kelly sits at a desk at home, preparing for a major test.

    B. Belief/Thought: Kelly thinks_____

    _____

    C. Consequence: Kelly begins to cry.

3. A. Situation: During a final examination, Sam keeps looking around the room at other students busily answering test questions.

    B. Belief/Thought: Sam thinks_____

    _____

    C. Consequence: Sam goes blank and starts to perspire.

Many of us, when asked if we have negative or unproductive thoughts, would answer "Not me! I'm an upbeat sort of person." Still, most of us occasionally feel down, angry, hurt or some other unpleasant emotion. Negative thoughts always precede the unpleasant emotions.

Exercise 2
Identify Your Own Thought Patterns

To identify your own patterns of thinking, carry a small notebook or use the notes section in your phone for the next week. Every time you experience any unpleasant emotion, write down the situation, what you thought and your reaction. You will probably find that the same type of negative self-talk repeats and repeats in your brain.

After one week, return to this section and answer the question below.

Analyze & Adjust

Identify Your Own Thought Patterns

What did you learn during this week about the relationship between your thoughts and your feelings? Did you discover any patterns?

_____

_____

_____

_____

After completing this exercise one student discovered his trigger was the phrase, "Oh crap!" When he made a mistake and thought, "Oh crap!" he then began a diatribe against himself, reminding himself of every mistake he'd ever made. Once he recognized the thought that caused the negative thinking, he was able to stop it.

⟩⟩ Persuade Yourself to Discard Unproductive Thoughts

If you have developed the habit of a certain type of unproductive thinking, it may take some work for you to give it up. You have just spent a week analyzing how your own emotions may be related to your thoughts. If you have identified a persistent thought that causes you trouble, you can put that thought to the test _now_.

First, ask, **"Is it true?"** Let's imagine, for example, that you have an unproductive thought of the "I'm not good enough" variety. If you are in college, clearly some people thought you had a good chance to succeed, or you would not have been admitted. It may be true that the college curriculum is more difficult than courses you took in high school, and you have to work harder now in order to succeed. Most of the other students in your classes are probably working harder now than they did in their previous course work. So, a good replacement thought might be, "This may be harder than other classes have been, but I will just have to work harder." That statement would have quite different emotional and behavioral consequences, wouldn't it?

Second, ask yourself, even if there is some grain of truth in the statement (that is, failure is possible), **"Is it useful"** to say this to myself while I am studying or taking an exam? The answer to that question is a resounding, "No!"

Lastly, does thinking negatively help you **achieve your goals** in life? Again, "No." No matter what your goals, negative thinking can only put stumbling blocks in your way. If your unproductive thoughts lead to unhappiness and physical symptoms of stress, they are certainly not helping you along the path you've chosen for your life.

We hope that asking yourself these three questions about your negative thoughts will convince you to change the thought to one that is true, useful and gets you where you want to go in life.

Replace Unproductive Thoughts

If unproductive thinking is occasionally making you feel depressed, anxious or worried, you can learn to change to more productive thinking. You can become happier, calmer, more energetic, more motivated and more confident by replacing negative thoughts with positive thoughts that are also realistic.

The replacement thoughts cannot be unbelievable, or you'll quickly discard them and go right back to the original negative thought. If you were thinking, "I'm going to fail the test," you can't simply say, "I'm going to get a perfect score!" You will not believe the new thought. But you *could* say, "I'm going to do my best. I'm going to give it my best shot." That is an entirely realistic idea and will lead to feeling more motivated—a feeling that is useful when you have to put out a lot of effort reviewing for a test.

Finding useful replacement thoughts may not be easy at first. Below are some ideas to help you get started.

Four Tips for Choosing Replacement Thoughts

1. Use only *positive* words in the replacement thought. For example, if you are thinking "I am going to fail this test," you would not replace it with "I won't fail this test." The words "won't" and "fail" are both negative. It would be better to say something about how much effort you are putting into studying or how much your studying is improving. For example, "I am working hard at my studies," or "I'm improving my study habits."

2. If you can't come up with something positive in the situation, try for something that at least is *neutral*. For example, "I am getting better," or "I am trying harder."

3. Make sure you *believe* your replacement thought. For example, try something along the lines of "Most of the class will pass the test, so I probably will, too." It's enough to point yourself in the direction you want to go.

4. How many positive thoughts do you need? There is actually a ratio to help you track your positive to negative comments, which for our purposes we will apply to your self talk. It's called the "Positivity to Negativity Ratio." The ideal ratio is three positive comments to every one negative comment in a work setting and five positive comments for every one negative comment at home, with family members and close friends. But there is also an upper limit. People who make more than 12 positive comments for every one negative comment are typically not believed.

Replace Your Unproductive Thoughts—as Easy as A. B. C. D.

One student kept telling himself that the information he was studying for a certain course would never be of any use to him after graduation. Saying that to himself made him feel annoyed, ("What a waste of time!") and often led to avoiding studying that subject. After he identified his negative thought, he replaced it by telling himself, "Maybe there's a good reason they want us to learn this. I'll probably find out later where this information fits in when I take other courses. Then I'll be glad I learned it," or, "I like to learn new stuff."

If you identified any unproductive thoughts in the exercise earlier in the chapter, the next part of the chapter will be helpful.

Do the exercise below in the five to seven days preceding a test. The stress of preparing for a test is likely to make your favorite negative thought recur. You will be doing this exercise repeatedly, because negative thinking patterns are often deeply rooted habits, and repetition will be required to remove them. The repetition may seem a little boring, but boring is good. Boring is at least not anxiety, quite the opposite. Over that week, you should have talked yourself out of your useless negative thought. Here's what to do every time the unproductive thought appears.

Exercise 3
Replace Thoughts by Arguing with Yourself

Directions: Use the "Replace Unproductive Thoughts" worksheet to complete this exercise.

First, identify the situation, which will be labeled 'A.' Then say aloud the bothersome thought 'B.' This keeps the thought from lurking unnoticed and brings it out into the open. For example, you might say out loud, "There's no way I'm going to pass that

Exercise 3
Replace Unproductive Thoughts

A. Activating event: Situation in which the thought occurs.

_____

_____

B. Belief or bothersome thought in that situation:

_____

_____

C. Consequence: (can be emotional or behavioral or both)

_____

_____

D. Dispute and decide: Is the belief *true*? *useful*? and will it
   help me get where I want to go?

_____

_____

Replacement thought/belief: _____

_____

_____

_____

_____

statistics test next week." In saying it aloud, or writing it down,
you are, as it were, facing down the enemy.

Next, think about how you feel or act whenever you have that
thought. Does it make you tense, depressed and avoid looking at

your statistics text or notes? C stands for "consider the consequences." Write the consequences of your belief under C.

Third, go through the three questions.

> Is it *true* that you can't possibly pass your statistics exam? Or is your self-talk an exaggeration?

> Is it *useful* to keep telling yourself this unproductive message? Not likely. It makes you feel bad in any number of ways.

> Will it help you pass the test (*achieve your goal*) to keep saying that to yourself? Certainly not.

'D' is for 'dispute and decide.'

So, if you decide to replace the "I can't pass" thought with something more useful and also believable. Write your decision after "D" on the worksheet.

Finally, write your replacement thought in the last blank and repeat it to yourself every time the negative thought recurs. A helpful replacement thought might be something like, "I will do my best," or "I will take lots of practice tests to prepare for the exam next week."

Short Cut

Once you have done the hard work and learned to be aware of negative or unproductive thinking, you may be able to take a short-cut to getting rid of that thought. Some people find that physical movement can help them discard a thought and reorient their thinking.

Have you ever seen a person quickly shake her head when she's heard or thought something unpleasant? That's a gesture you can use. A simple physical change like sitting down or standing up, a shake of the head or putting your hands to your face can be your signal to change channels in your thinking. Even moving your eyes—literally shifting your focus to a different object—can help change the way you look at things.

Analyze & Adjust

Replace Unproductive Thoughts

Briefly describe what you have learned about identifying and replacing unproductive thoughts. Is this something that is easy or difficult for you to do?

_____

_____

_____

_____

Another Approach to Self-Talk—Growth Mindset

In a 2012 interview, Carol Dweck, author of the book *Mindset,* said:

> In a fixed mindset students believe their basic abilities, their intelligence, their talents, are just fixed traits. They have a certain amount and that's that, and then their goal becomes to look smart all the time and never look dumb. In a growth mindset students understand that their talents and abilities can be developed through effort, good teaching and persistence. They don't necessarily think everyone's the same or anyone can be Einstein, but they believe everyone can get smarter if they work at it.

Below is a table based on information from page 245 in the book *Mindset.* This table summarizes the two mindsets discussed in the book and how each of them responds to life events. Work towards creating a growth mindset.

Table 6.1   Fixed vs. Growth Mindset

	Fixed Mindset	Growth Mindset
Challenges	Avoids challenges	**Embraces challenges**
Obstacles	Gets defensive. Gives up easily	**Persists in the face of setbacks**
Effort	Sees effort as fruitless or worse	**Sees effort as the path to mastery**
Cricicism	Ignores useful negative feedback	**Learns from criticism**
Success of others	Feels threatened by the success of others	**Finds lessons and inspiration in the success of others**

Mastery = Moving From Negativity to Enjoyment

Perhaps you don't get enough exercise, because you think exercise routines are boring. You can go on beyond neutral, which could be something like, "I'll feel better after I exercise today." You can get to positively enjoying your workout. You can think, "No day is complete until I've had my exercise," or "It feels so good to move. I love my daily walks!"

You can get past neutral to positive with studying and test-taking, too. You can actually look forward to a pleasant evening of reading your assignments. You can take delight in creating a beautiful set of notes. Attractive notes are a joy to behold. When you learn to feel happy for the opportunity to show what you have learned as you take a test, you will have become a world-class positive thinker.

The book *Change Anything* (2011) by Patterson, Grenny, Maxfield, McMillan & Switzler, has a chapter called, Love What You Hate (47–65). The chapter discusses the steps for changing your thinking and behavior. Their approach is similar to what is discussed in this step on self-talk, but if you'd like to further improve, you may want to read it.

QUIZ Physical Symptoms of Anxiety

Physical symptoms can also help you identify negative, unproductive thinking. These symptoms can interfere with studying, learning and test-taking. If the ABCD approach does not work to quell the physical symptoms, you may want to see if the counseling center offers training to help minimize the distractions of anxiety. Often, relaxation training is taught in conjunction with guided imagery. This is typically in a group, class-like setting.

Put a check mark in front of any or all of the physical symptoms that sometimes or often apply to you just prior to or during an exam.

___ Skin flushing or rash

___ Hands trembling or unsteady legs

___ Nausea

___ Chest pain

___ Ragged breathing

___ Dizziness

___ Difficulty swallowing or dry mouth

___ Chills

___ Rapid heart rate

___ Excessive perspiration

___ Headache

___ Neck or back pain

If any of the above symptoms of physical tension occur regularly immediately preceding and/or during exams, go to your school health and counseling center. The staff can probably provide some form of relaxation training, either individually, as a group, or with a recording. Feeling anxious, especially in a testing situation, is so common for students that school counseling centers typically offer a variety of programs to deal with it.

Decades of research attest to the success of these anxiety reduction programs. School counseling centers are offered as a service to you, usually without any charge, so you might as well take advantage of them. There are also a myriad of books and recordings that you can find online or check out from libraries and use whenever anxiety causes physical discomfort.

You might be interested to know that research published in the June 26, 2013, issue of the *Journal of Neuroscience* states that lack of adequate sleep can exacerbate feelings of anxiety and anxiety disorders. "The study suggests that innate worriers . . . are acutely vulnerable to the impact of sleep loss."

Meanwhile, use the physical symptoms as clues to when you are having a problematic thought. You may be unaware of the underlying thought, but it's hard to ignore trembling hands or the sudden onset of nausea.

Exercise 4
Make Encouragement Cards

Encouragement cards are notes or cards on which you have written statements that are true, useful and help move you closer to your goals. Make your own encouragement cards and post them near your study area or any other place where you will see them often.

Analyze & Adjust
Check-Up on Exercise 4
Encouragement Cards

1. What did you learn from making, posting and reading your Encouragement Cards?

_____

_____

2. Were you able to reduce or eliminate some of your negative thoughts? Say more about that.

_____

_____

3. Write about some of the changes you have made as a result of working through this book.

_____

_____

_____

_____

4. Go back to Start Here, the Current Study Strategies section, and compare your present study strategies to your old ones. Have you made any changes? What productive and helpful comments might your best friend say to you about the changes you have made to how you approach your studies?

_____

_____

_____

_____

_____

_____

⟫ Summary

Much anxiety is the result of unconscious thinking. Bringing those unproductive thoughts to the surface—raising them to consciousness—and replacing them with more beneficial thinking will help relieve anxiety and lessen or eliminate physical symptoms of stress.

Your campus counseling center may offer group classes or individual sessions on dealing with different types of anxiety. There are many proven ways to reduce the symptoms and causes of anxiety. Reach out to those who are trained in this area so you can learn how to manage unproductive thoughts and feelings and feel happier.

⟫ References

Baumeister, R.F., Heatherton, T.F., & Tice, D.M. (1994). *Losing control: How and why people fail at self-regulation*. San Diego, CA: Academic Press.

> The authors have synthesized the research on self-regulation failure. They briefly discuss the relationship between self-esteem and self-regulation and hypothesize that lack of self-regulation may lead to lack of self-esteem. They conclude that capacity for self-regulation can be increased with effective practice.

Brooks, M. (2013). Sleep disruption a key factor in anxiety disorders. *Medscape Medical News.*
http://www.medscape.com/viewarticle/807404?src

Dweck Interview. (2012). Stanford University's Carol Dweck on the Growth Mindset and Education. http://onedublin.org/2012/06/19/stanford-universitys-carol-dweck-on-the-growth-mindset-and-education/

Dweck, C.S. (2006). *Mindset: The new psychology of success.* NY: Ballantine Books.

Eliot, J. (2004). *Overachievement: The new model for exceptional performance.* NY: Portfolio.

Eliot teaches that overachieving means thriving under pressure—welcoming it, enjoying it and make it work to your advantage.

Ellis, A. (1971). *Growth through reason.* Palo Alto, CA: Science and Behavior Books.

Ellis is the original guru of thought-stopping as a way to feel happier. His several books are written in a readable, humorous style. His work does not refer specifically to test anxiety but to living well by keeping negative thoughts under control.

Helmstetter, S. (1982). *What to say when you talk to yourself.* New York: Pocket Books.

Discusses the five levels of Self Talk and gives specific word-for-word recommendations for constructing productive self talk. Also discusses the effectiveness of internal motivation as opposed to external motivation.

Hembrie, R. (1988). Correlates, causes, effects, and treatment of test anxiety. *Review of Educational Research, 58,* 47–77.

A thorough review of 562 studies of test anxiety. Author concludes that test anxiety can reduce test scores and also that test anxiety is correlated with negative self-evaluations and lower self-esteem.

Howard, P.J. (2000). *The owner's manual for the brain: Everyday applications from mind-brain research.* (2nd ed.) Atlanta: Bard Press.

Chapter 20 is about Motivation, Stress and Burnout. It reviews research of each, and encourages the reader to take charge of his or her life. Includes Martin Seligman's research from the book *Learned Optimism.*

Maultsby, M. (1975). *Help yourself to happiness*. New York: Institute of Rational Emotive Therapy.

A good introduction to thought control for the general reader. Maultsby was a student of Ellis' earlier work.

Patterson, K., Grenny, J., Maxfield, D., McMillan, R. and Switzler, A. (2011). *Change anything: The new science of personal success*. NY: Business Plus/Hachette Book Group.

Positivity/Negativity Ratio: based in the work of: Marcial Losada (business) & John Gottman (marriage) & Barbara Fredrickson (positive psychology) http://happierhuman.com/losada-ratio/

Seligman, M.E.P. (2011). *Flourish: A visionary new understanding of happiness and well-being*. NY: Simon & Schuster.

Standard deviation diagram. By Mwtoews - Own work, based (in concept) on figure by Jeremy Kemp, on 2005-02-09. Licensed under Creative Commons Attribution 2.5 via Wikimedia Commons. http://commons.wikimedia.org/wiki/File:Standard_deviation_diagram.svg#mediaviewer/File:Standard_deviation_diagram.svg

Next Steps

You've come a long way in just six steps! You have learned *how* to learn.

Managing your time, being prepared, organizing and recalling information—these are life skills! Continue to practice these strategies as you move forward. You'll be amazed at how useful they are.

And remember grit? If you didn't have grit when you started this adventure, you probably have it now. Perseverance is highly correlated with success in many areas of life, not just in college.

We would enjoy hearing from you!

You may contact us at sixsteps2@gmail.com or our website at www.VitalStudySkills.com or www.SixStepsToCollegeSuccess.com

Thank you for allowing us to share this part of your journey.

Wishing you all the best,

—Kathleen C. Straker
—Eugenia G. Kelman

p.s. In the following pages we've added a Bonus section to help you apply these strategies to classroom and standardized exams.

Bonus Material

How to Take a Test

Does it seem like there is always a test coming up? There is. If you are taking five courses and each course has a total of three exams, that means a minimum of fifteen exams over a 15–16 week period. So yes, there always is a test around the corner. But if you are following the steps in this book you will have a weekly schedule that allows time to get everything done without cramming or all-nighters.

Think of test-taking as if it is a sport and you are an elite athlete. Before a competition would you stay up all night? Eat unhealthy food? Overdose on caffeine or any other drug? Not if you wanted to win! Be sensible and take good care of your health—especially prior to exams.

Four Phases of Test Preparation

1. Content

Many students assume that if they have mastered the content they are well prepared. That is the first and most important component, but it's not the only one.

2. Test Wise

Nearly as important as mastering the content is becoming test wise. We use the term test wise to mean becoming familiar with the types of questions (straight multiple choice, long passages with a series of questions, essay); the testing software (are you allowed to skip questions and move around in a section, do incorrect answers count against you); and the testing environment (is scratch paper provided, are ear plugs allowed; does the computer use a mouse or a touch pad).

Computer versions of tests may allow you to skip around as you would on a paper-and-pencil exam, or they may require you to answer questions in a linear fashion, starting with question number one and answering each item, in order, through the entire exam. The computer administered test may require you to use an on-screen calculator, so scratch paper may not be allowed. Before the exam date, check the course syllabus or ask your professor if the test will be paper-and-pencil or computer based, so you can plan your practice sessions and test-taking strategy accordingly.

3. Emotional

Emotional preparation is especially important during the time you are learning the content and when you are answering practice question. Use productive self talk to stay motivated and focused while preparing for the exam and on test day.

4. Physical

Though it may seem counter-intuitive, it is important to be physically fit, (including well rested and well nourished) when you must sit and concentrate during an exam.

❱❱ A Day or Two Before a Test

If you are working with a quiz group, plan your final review 24-48 hours before the exam. You may discover that you forgot to study a topic. A day or two will give you time to learn the material without stress. Discovering a gap in your knowledge just an hour or two before an exam can be quite unnerving!

Assuming you are following the steps in this book, you will already have seen the information a number of times before the test. You will probably need just one final review. Whether or not to self-test at this point depends on how much anxiety self-testing might create. If you would become a quivering bundle of nerves, don't do it. The study system taught in this book makes cramming unnecessary. Your knowledge and understanding of the information at this point should get you easily through the test, even when you have to make educated guesses.

)) Immediately Before a Test

Avoid groups of students who are doing last-second reviews. This can be very anxiety producing. Even if you know the material well, you may inadvertently pick up on some of their nervousness. Find a quiet place where you can do some slow, deep breathing to calm yourself or even look over your notes, if you can do so calmly.

)) During a Test

Keeping Track of Time

When you first begin your test, take a minute to do two things: 1) write down from memory any formulas or equations you may need to refer to during the test and 2) decide how much time you should spend (on average) per item and at what item number you should be at the half-way point of the time allowed for the test. If it is a paper-and-pencil exam, your calculation should allow five to ten minutes at the end to return to unanswered items to see if you need to guess or can make a more informed answer at that time. So, if you have 60 minutes to complete the test, and the test consists of 50 items, you can give yourself one minute per item and still have ten minutes to go back to unanswered items.

Some items take less than a minute; some take more. You should stay close to the average as you work through the test and

definitely get to the mid-point on time. Answer all the easy questions first. This will build your confidence and make sure you get points for the answers you know. In most multiple-choice tests, all the items have the same point value, so it is not advantageous to miss an easy item just because you spent too much time on a hard one. If some questions count for more points, however, your strategy may be to answer the highest value questions first.

If you are taking a paper-and-pencil exam, make an obvious mark in the margin for any difficult item you decide to skip in the interest of saving time. The check mark will help you find this item quickly when you return to it. Attentive test-takers often notice that some information or cue in a later item reminds them of the answer to an earlier item they skipped.

Working an Item Using the True, False, ? Approach

Following is a list of all possible responses to any option:

T = I know this is true
F = I know this is false
?T = I think this is true, but I'm not sure
?F = I think this is false, but I'm not sure
? = I haven't got a clue

Have you ever read a through a list of options only to forget the first option by the time you got to the last one? This strategy can help you keep track of what you are thinking as you read and consider each one. As you read the options on a multiple-choice question, write T, F, ?T, ?F, or ? in the margin next to the number or letter, according to the system as described above. This will help you keep track of your thinking as you work through the item and avoid marking a choice you didn't intend.

Careless Errors

Especially if you are using a Scantron® form, periodically check that the number you are marking corresponds to the test item you are answering. If you check every ten items, you'll have fewer items to erase if you get off the numbering sequence. Just check that every time an item ends in zero, (10, 20, 30, etc.) the number on the answer sheet also ends in zero. Imagine your distress if you wait until the end and discover you are bubbling item 59 on a 60-item test! Even worse, that you got out of sync with the bubble sheet back at item 5! You could have to erase everything and hope you have time to correct them all, beg the teacher to let you fix the problem, or possibly fail the exam.

Do not try to be the first one out of the classroom after the test. On your exam, use any gift of time to:

> Double-check that your answer sheet numbers and test item numbers correspond.

> Double-check that all items are answered *on the answer sheet.*

> If you still have extra time, re-read any items that you guessed at earlier. You may find that you originally mis-read part of a stem or option.

> But DO NOT, and we repeat, DO NOT change answers on a hunch. More on this below.

Changing Answers

When you have plenty of time to go back over the test and re-read items already answered, you may be tempted to change an answer. *Don't.* Don't change an answer merely on a hunch. Your first guess is typically better than your second guess. But the research suggests that you may change your answer if you have a good reason, for example, some new information that makes your original response incorrect.

Expect the Unexpected

Sometimes, despite excellent preparation, you will encounter unexpected topics or question formats on an exam. Has your instructor always given 50-item exams until this one? Now there are 60 questions to answer in the same amount of time! What to do? The first thing to do is to take a deep breath. Anxiety will not help. Now is the time for productive self-talk. Remind yourself that everyone else is in the same boat.

Concentrate on doing the best you can on each test item. Instead of using test time to ask your instructor about the unexpected changes, wait until after the test is over.

Tips for Improved Guessing on Classroom Exams

Use these strategies only when you have NO IDEA what the correct answer is.

1. If there is no penalty for guessing, do it. The directions for a test will tell you if points are subtracted for incorrect responses. In that case, you probably shouldn't guess, though some test experts have argued that the odds for guessing are still fairly good.

2. Repetition in the question and option can be a clue to the correct answer.

3. Specific determiners can be a hint when you have to guess. "Always," "never," "inevitably," and possibly "completely" are often clues to the incorrectness of a response option, because rarely are things so absolute.

4. Avoid answers with grammatical inconsistency between the question and the option or other grammar cues.

5. Avoid the absurd option. This may occasionally appear as a bit of levity offered by the teacher in a classroom test (but is highly unlikely in a standardized examination.)

6. Longer, more complicated or more complete options are often the correct answer.

7. Choose familiar options. Test questions are almost always based on information presented either in the lecture, text or both. It is not a good idea to choose an option that is completely unfamiliar.

8. Choose between similar options. Often, two options are alike except for one or two words, and the other options are all different. The answer is usually one of those two options.

9. Choose "good" or conscientious answers. When you haven't a clue, choose good things. A response option that seems more careful or conscientious should be considered "true."

10. On "true / false" questions choose "true" if you must guess. Statistically "true" is more often the correct answer than "false."

Out of Time

In the event that you run out of time on a classroom exam and must mark an answer without even reading the item, your best bet is to pick a single column and mark that column straight down to the end. You'll find you pick up more points by choosing one letter and just marking straight down. If you don't believe us, try it on an old exam answer sheet. Compare how many guesses are correct in the straight down the column method versus random bubbling.

)) What About Essay Questions?

Occasionally you will have to respond to an in-class question with a short essay. For example, in a history class you may be asked, "What were the difference between Abraham Lincoln and Stephen Douglas on two important slavery issues?"

If you had created a category chart as you studied this topic, you could quickly re-create it to answer this question.

Name	Party Affiliation	Dred Scott Decision	Compromise of 1850
Abraham Lincoln	Republican	Opposed the decision on moral grounds: a man is not property.	Disagreed. Did not believe it would work.
Stephen Douglas	Democrat	Initially agreed with decision but said popular sovereignty should govern each state's decision to allow slavery or not.	Co-wrote the compromise, based on the principle of popular sovereignty.

You could begin your essay based on this chart by pointing out that Lincoln's Republican position is used in the original meaning of the word "republic," whereas Douglas believed in the rule of popular vote. In the Dred Scott decision, Lincoln opposed and Douglas initially agreed, but said let the people decide in each state.

Using this chart, your essay practically writes itself. All you have to do is convert the information in the chart into complete sentences and you have a well-organized essay.

You can also write an essay from a flowchart. Here's an example from a course in geology.

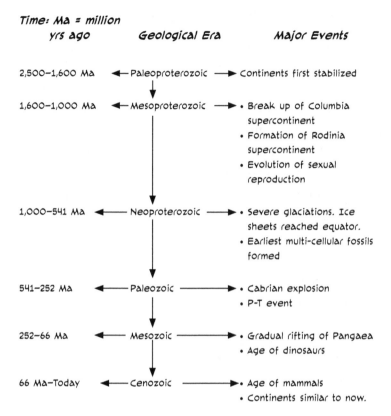

Time: Ma = million
 yrs ago   Geological Era   Major Events

2,500–1,600 Ma   ◄— Paleoproterozoic —► Continents first stabilized

1,600–1,000 Ma   ◄— Mesoproterozoic —► • Break up of Columbia
                                          supercontinent
                                        • Formation of Rodinia
                                          supercontinent
                                        • Evolution of sexual
                                          reproduction

1,000–541 Ma   ◄— Neoproterozoic —► • Severe glaciations. Ice
                                          sheets reached equator.
                                        • Earliest multi-cellular fossils
                                          formed

541–252 Ma   ◄— Paleozoic —► • Cabrian explosion
                                  • P-T event

252–66 Ma   ◄— Mesozoic —► • Gradual rifting of Pangaea
                                 • Age of dinosaurs

66 Ma–Today   ◄— Cenozoic —► • Age of mammals
                                 • Continents similar to now.

Of course, this could be a category chart, but nicely illustrates changes over time. Again, it's easy to write an essay from this flow chart just by turning the details into sentences. For example, your essay could begin:

"In the Paleoproterozoic era, 2,500–1,600 Ma, a significant event was the stabilization of the continents. This era was followed by . . . ."

)) If You Start Getting Tired During an Exam

Fatigue and hunger can lead to carelessness and leaving the exam early. To wake yourself from lethargy, try small exercises (that won't disturb your neighbors) like stretching your neck, raising your shoulders to your ears, making tight fists of your hands and releasing only after some tension builds. Deep breaths and tightening and then relaxing muscles can be refreshing. Exercising muscles in this way is not noisy and not very visible.

Find out if your teachers or exam proctors mind if you bring some energy-building food into the testing room, but avoid anything noisy (no carrot-chomping or crackling of paper, please). Nuts or dried fruits are a good choice and are easy to handle in the test situation. Better yet, eat a healthful meal immediately prior to the exam.

)) After a Test: It's Not Over Even When It's Over

Odds are that you missed a few items on the last test that you took. Learn from your mistakes! There is a great deal to discover when you are able to look over a graded exam. If you didn't do well on the exam you need to discover exactly what went wrong, so you can avoid making the same mistakes. It may not be pleasant to look at test errors, but doing so can help you improve future test scores. Plan to attend the post-test review if one is offered—even if you made a good grade. Comments made during the review session can help you learn how test questions are chosen, and that information will help you on future exams.

Did your lack of knowledge cause the error? If so, did you not have that information in your review notes? Why not? In our experience, this is the principle cause of missing points on tests. If you are often able to get the answer choices down to two options, but chose the incorrect one, that means there is another level of detail that you will need to learn. Are your notes detailed enough? Look back over them after a test to see if they are. If the missed items were in your notes, that means you need additional review and self-test. If the missed items were not in your notes, that means you need to make more detailed notes.

Did you miss the item due to lack of test-taking skills? This is probably the second most frequent cause, especially carelessness in reading the item.

Were you so nervous that you didn't think straight during the exam? Were you so physically ill that you couldn't function during the exam? Faculty usually have an alternative testing plan

Worksheet 8.1   Test Error Analysis

Item # of question missed	Lack of knowl- edge? Yes/No	Was info in notes? Yes/No	Did I review the info? Yes/No	Did I self-test on the info? Yes/No	Was it a test- taking error? Yes/No	If yes, what type of test- taking error?

for a student who is seriously ill. Find out what it is before you need it!

Finally, do not let a single bad test score get you down. What is done is done, and you must focus on the next exam. Do not let frustration derail your study plans. You have a solid study system in place, so learn from each exam how to do better on the next one.

The Test Error Analysis worksheet will help you analyze the reasons for missing items on a test. Complete the table then analyze the information. Do you see any patterns? What conclusions can you draw about your test-preparation strategies?

After your next exam you can see how well the components of this system work for you by completing the Test Error Analysis worksheet. If an area needs further improvement, re-read that step and re-work the related exercises.

Prepare for Entrance Exams

Not only will the Six Steps help you excel in your college studies, you can use these same strategies to help you excel on entrance or other standardized exams. If you plan to continue your education after college, you will likely be required to take one of the following:

> Allied Health Professions Admission Test (AHPAT)

> Dental Admission Test (DAT)

> Graduate Management Admission Test (GMAT)

> Graduate Record Examination (GRE)

> Law School Admission Test (LSAT)

> Miller Analogies Test (MAT)

> Medical College Admission Test (MCAT)

> Optometry Admission Test (OAT)

> Pharmacy College Admission Test (PCAT)

)) Planning Your 3- to 4-Month Review Schedule

Depending on how much time you have each week to devote to exam prep, you will probably need to begin your review three to four months before the exam date. Even if you are not taking classes or working, we recommend that you plan no more than four hours per day of intensive study. Research with elite athletes and musicians has found that the amount of concentration required to focus intently cannot be sustained much longer than a total of four hours per day, so we make a similar recommendation. This is not four consecutive hours, but a total of four hours broken into 30, 60, 90 or 120 minute periods, with breaks in between.

If you have three months (12 weeks) to prepare, studying six days a week for four hours per day will give you 288 hours of preparation. If you have four months (16 weeks) to prepare, six days per week, four hours per day, will give you 384 hours of preparation.

So, if you have twelve to sixteen weeks to prepare, you will need to spend approximately 24 hours per week. If you have eight weeks to prepare then you will need to spend approximately 36 hours per week, but this would require six hours per day, which is more than the recommended four hours. If you have less than eight weeks to prepare you might want to consider finding another testing date to allow time for adequate preparation.

Some students prefer to schedule their study days by topics, rather than by the number of hours they plan to study. That is all right if you keep in mind that periods of concentrated attention will increase your recall. Staring at the same page for an hour "trying to understand it" is not an efficient or effective use of your time.

Your standardized exam preparation will provide another opportunity for you to use your category charts, flowcharts, diagrams and note cards. If you have created those notes and studied from them before, it will make reviewing and remembering what is on them much easier than using all new study materials.

Preparation Tips

> Review the Four Phases of Test Preparation in the previous How to Take a Test section.

> Pace yourself. If you will be spending several months or weeks in preparation, design a schedule that is sustainable for that period of time.

> The last few weeks of preparation for a high-stakes exam is *not* the time to begin a fast or make radical changes to your diet.

Standardized Exam Scores and Course Grades

Standardized exam scores are typically highly correlated with course grades. Begin planning your review schedule by looking back at the relevant courses you have taken in your current program of study. This will require some candid self assessment on your part.

We recommend you begin your period of review with the topic that is *most difficult* for you (which is likely where you received your lowest grades) and work towards the topics or areas that come more easily. By using this approach you will ensure that you spend time on the areas that need the most work. If you run out of time as you near the exam date, you'll be glad you didn't neglect your weaker areas to spend more time on your strong subjects. The point is to spend more time where you need the most review and spend less time where you need less review.

How to Use Practice Questions and Practice Exams

Most standardized exams are now given only in computer administered formats. Make sure you are intimately acquainted with the types of questions and formats used. Learn what the "standard testing conditions" include and prepare for those. For example, will you be given paper and pencil to use during the exam or a small white board and marker? Are ear plugs allowed?

Will the computer have a mouse or a touch pad? Find out from the test administrator or testing site and practice accordingly.

Using questions as your *only* review tool will *not* provide the structure necessary to pinpoint how to best spend your time. Most review materials have short (10–20) sets of questions that are well-suited for self-testing over a specific topic. The longer tests (50–200 questions) can be used as practice tests (these should cover material from all the topics on which you will be tested) and taken once or twice a week during your review period. Some exam preparation programs recommend that by the time you sit for the actual exam, you should have answered 2,000–3,000 practice-exam questions.

The pages that follow will give you step-by-step instructions in how to prepare for your standardized exam. You may choose to use it as a checklist and mark the "Done" column as you complete each task.

You've labored long and hard toward this goal, so keep up the great work!

A note about keeping yourself motivated. Every day give yourself a small reward to look forward to. The best kind of reward is one that gets you up and moving, perhaps taking a walk with a friend. Each week choose a slightly larger reward that you can look forward to. The secret to rewarding yourself is to make sure that the reward doesn't derail your study goals. (Staying up all night to socialize would not be considered a good choice, since you'll be sleep deprived afterwards.)

A Step-by-Step Guide to Preparing for Your Entrance Exam

Action to Take	Done
Scheduling Time	
Go to the exam website to view the list of exam dates. If possible, choose a test date at or near the end of a break, so you will have time to study for the exam without other academic commitments. (For example at the end of the summer or winter break.)	
On the monthly section of your calendar, mark off any dates you cannot study between now and the proposed exam date.	
Beginning with the proposed exam date, count <u>backwards</u> the number of days available between the exam and the start of your review. If you are planning on 3–4 months of preparation, the available number of study days should be between 72 and 96 days. How many hours on each of those days will you be able to study? Will that add up to the 288–384 hours recommended?	
Make sure you leave at least seven to ten days prior to the exam open, with nothing scheduled. This will allow time for a general review of the material and will give you a little flex time in case an emergency arises that gets you off track for a few days.	
Plan & Prepare	
Decide what resources will be most useful.	
Will some of the material come from college courses you have already taken? If so, locate and organize your text books and class notes by subject. Make a list of every relevant course and the grade received (and test grades, if you have that information.) Based on this information, list areas to review. Begin with the one that needs the most work (i.e., has the lowest grade and is worth the most points on the exam), second is the next lowest and so on.	
Do you need to buy or borrow review materials?	
Purchase or borrow one or two review books, preferably with access to additional online practice questions. Choose a resource that you hear is more difficult than the others.	
If you have access to practice exams that closely simulate the actual standardized exam, take a diagnostic exam and use the data from the practice exam to help you plan your review schedule. (Again, starting with the area that needs the most work.)	
Revise Your Schedule	
Now that you have a better idea of how you will need to spend your time (after taking a diagnostic exam), go back to your calendar and fill in the weekly and daily activities, writing exactly what you plan to do each day to accomplish your weekly goals.	

Continues on next page

A Step-by-Step Guide, *continued*

Action to Take	Done
Read & Make Notes for Review & Self-Test	
Beginning with your weakest topic, estimate the time you will allocate to each topic area. The activities that will be included in your study and review sessions for each topic may vary, but should include most of these elements: 1. Review your old charts, cards, notes or review sources 2. Read and make study notes on any content material not yet mastered 3. Self-test over your own notes 4. Take a short 10–20 question quiz 5. Review responses to practice test questions 6. Read and make notes to fill in any knowledge gaps 7. Take a full-length practice test 8. Review responses to full-length practice test 9. Is the topic is mastered? (85% or higher on practice quizzes and tests). If not, write the name of the topic and materials to use for further review on the "Final Review List" 10. Repeat steps above as time allows and then move on to the next topic	
Online practice questions will typically give you feedback on the type of question and content area. We suggest that you create a tracking grid to record the topics that have been reviewed and learned to the 85% criterion, as well as a record of the topics that need additional review and practice.	
Once you have estimated the time you want to spend on each topic, re-count how many days and hours your review schedule allows. Is it enough? Do you need to change the start date for your review or the test date?	
On your schedule each day write: • topics to review • amount of time (hours) for each • the score of your practice exams—by subject area • rewards for getting your work accomplished	
Once you have reached at least 85% mastery of the content, move on to the next topic. If you have used all the time that you allowed for that topic, you will need to either adjust your schedule to borrow a few hours from another topic and spend a little more time on that area now, or plan to add it to your "Final Review List" and come back to it during your final review in the week before the exam. **Suggestion:** It's usually better to move on and not get bogged down in one area, unless it is absolutely fundamental to everything else you will be studying.	

Action to Take	Done
Self Test	
In addition to the daily or weekly quizzes you will be taking, plan to space at least six to ten full-length practice tests (100+ questions) throughout your review period. This will let you know how effective your study/review system is and will still allow adequate time to remediate any areas that need further work. Schedule your last full-length practice test one to two weeks before the actual exam. You will continue to study, review and self-test during those last two weeks, but do not plan to take a full length practice test in the last several days before the "real" one, so you won't be burned out.	
The last one to two weeks before the exam will be primarily spent preparing yourself physically and psychologically for the exam. While you may continue review of any topics on your "Final Review List" you will now be diligent about eating healthful foods, drinking plenty of water, moderate exercise and plenty of sleep. Your self-talk should consist of reminding yourself how well prepared you are for the exam and how you look forward to "showing what you know."	

Application Tips

In case you haven't already been advised to do so, create a professional email address for the application process. This is not the time to use your *BewareLordVoldemort* address. Your name and perhaps a number will show you can present yourself in a professional manner.

Most applications are pages and pages long and look overwhelming. Break the process into bite-sized pieces and work on it for short spans of time, once or twice a day, for one to two weeks and it will be completed in a timely manner and you will not be stressed out in the process.

About the Authors

Kathleen Straker, MEd, works with students from around the globe through her learning strategies workshops and individual academic coaching sessions. She also consults with faculty in course development and improving student retention. Ms. Straker is President of The Straker Group, LLC, a consulting firm based in Houston, Texas. This is her third book.

Eugenia Kelman, PhD, is a cognitive-behavioral psychologist. She has served on the faculty and in the administration at Colorado State University in Ft. Collins, CO; The University of Texas Medical Branch, Galveston, TX; and at Cornell University in Ithaca, NY. Her favorite question is, "What can I learn from this?"

About the Illustrator

Tammy Dubinsky grew up in Ardrossan, Alberta, Canada. It was here that her mom taught her how to draw apple trees and fences in proper perspective. Tammy graduated from the Alberta College of Art & Design, where she received a Bachelor of Design. She also completed the classical animation program at the Vancouver Film School. She now primarily animates for television. Tammy loves to draw and is very grateful to be able to do it for a living.

CPSIA information can be obtained
at www.ICGtesting.com
Printed in the USA
LVHW012343201118
597864LV00008B/152/P